P9-AGU-098

The New York Times

PIECE OF CAKE CROSSWORDS
Easy, Enjoyable Puzzles

Edited by Will Shortz

ST. MARTIN'S GRIFFIN ❦ NEW YORK

THE NEW YORK TIMES PIECE OF CAKE CROSSWORDS.
Copyright © 2006 by The New York Times Company. All rights reserved.
Printed in the United States of America. No part of this book may be
used or reproduced in any manner whatsoever without written
permission except in the case of brief quotations embodied
in critical articles or reviews. For information, address
St. Martin's Press, 175 Fifth Avenue, New York, N.Y. 10010.

www.stmartins.com

All of the puzzles that appear in this work were originally published
in the *New York Times* from June 29, 2004, to February 8, 2006.
Copyright © 2004, 2006 by The New York Times Company.
All Rights Reserved. Reprinted by permission.

ISBN-13: 978-0-312-36124-2
ISBN-10: 0-312-36124-6

10 9 8 7 6 5 4 3 2

The New York Times

PIECE OF CAKE CROSSWORDS

ACROSS
1 Basics
5 Raft wood
10 Goes (for)
14 Christine ___ (29-Down's love)
15 Leave stranded by a winter storm
16 One who says "I say, old chap"
17 See 11-Down
18 It crashes in 29-Down/60-Across
20 Seethes
22 Reverse of WNW
23 Site of Margaret Mead studies
24 With 40- and 51-Across, composer of 29-Down/60-Across, as well as 63-Across
26 Position
27 End a suit
30 Oboist's need
31 ___ Stadium, home of the U.S. Open
32 Theater areas
36 Old spy org.
39 Addict
40 See 24-Across
41 Aware of
42 Slice (off)
43 Toy gun ammo
44 Condo, e.g.
45 When repeated, words of agreement
47 Communion tables
49 Famed fireman Red
51 See 24-Across
54 Buddhist temple sights
55 "___ had it!"
56 Persistently worry
60 See 29-Down

63 Longest-running show in Broadway history until 1/9/06
64 Cheer (for)
65 Painter Matisse
66 Real name of 29-Down
67 West Point team
68 Hot, blue spectral type
69 Salon supplies

DOWN
1 Attaches
2 Can of worms?
3 Spelunking site
4 Brine
5 Pen name
6 One who's sore
7 Place for a renter's signature
8 Tendon
9 Now ___ then
10 Flattened at the poles
11 Carlotta, in 29-Down/60-Across
12 Fasten, as a ribbon
13 Costly strings
19 Twisty curves
21 NBC fixture since '75
25 Casino worker
27 Fellow named Bellow
28 Petrol provider
29 With 60-Across, longest-running show in Broadway history as of 1/9/06
30 Levi's jeans brand
33 Indisposed
34 Peruvian money
35 Soap ingredient
37 Cookbook direction
38 Tipplers
41 Went faster than
43 Examine grammatically
46 You might get a ticket for doing this
48 Novelist Deighton
49 Old marketplace
50 Help with
51 Wetnaps, e.g.
52 Happening
53 Quotable Yogi
57 Indiana city near Chicago
58 Play to ___
59 Sounds of disapproval
61 "So there you are!"
62 Put on TV

by David J. Kahn

2 WEDNESDAY

ACROSS

1 Dismay
6 Like flags
10 Rap sheet letters
13 Ragú rival
14 Native Canadian
15 Hasty escape
16 Tchaikovsky overture
19 Carrier to Europe
20 S ___ sugar
21 Former Georgia senator Sam
22 Frost-covered
24 Boiling point of water on the Celsius scale
28 Noted painter of flowers
30 Opposite end of the point
31 Composer Franck
32 Best Picture of 1958
33 Number of plays attributed to William Shakespeare
38 "Rats!"
39 Decorative pitchers
42 "___ Mucho"
45 Can't-miss proposition
47 Heinz tally of flavors
49 "Star Trek" helmsman
50 Fuji film competitor
51 "What ___ can I say?"
53 Test site

54 Sum of 16-, 24-, 33- and 47-Across
59 Plane domain
60 Brewer's kiln
61 Staring intently
62 Growing fig.?
63 Squeaks (out)
64 Flying Pan

DOWN

1 Boorish
2 Most stiffly proper
3 Good baseball throw
4 Turkish title
5 Much
6 Locale
7 Directional suffix
8 Freshly painted
9 Fresh
10 Fascination
11 Julie known as the voice of Marge Simpson
12 Fix
17 Article in Die Zeit
18 Extremes
19 Former McDonald's head Ray
23 "Woo-hoo!"
25 "___ an Englishman" ("H.M.S. Pinafore" song)
26 Impel
27 Less worldly
29 Islamic Sabbath
32 Ob-___
34 Butts
35 Koala's hangout
36 Pasture parents
37 Convert to a fine spray
40 Salon treatment
41 One-inch pencil, for example
42 V.I.P.
43 Physical exertion
44 Photo repro
45 Ward of "The Fugitive," 1993
46 Open with a pop
47 Political party in Palestine
48 Sleeveless garments
52 Barely beat
55 Make a bed?
56 Furniture wood
57 Homonym for 36-Down
58 Convened

by Mel Rosen

ACROSS

1 Persistent annoyer
5 Upper or lower bed
9 Monastery head
14 Author Wiesel
15 Geometry calculation
16 Does a prelaundry chore
17 Leader of an 1831 slave rebellion
19 "___ or treat?"
20 Rejects, as a lover
21 "That's ___" (Dean Martin classic)
23 1960's–70's singer Hayes
24 Bottom line, businesswise
28 Dobbin's doc
29 Actresses Graff and Kristen
31 "___ number one!" (stadium chant)
32 Suffix with Brooklyn
33 Meat that's often served piccata
34 Tête topper
35 Faultfinder extraordinaire
38 1988 Summer Olympics city
41 It may be kicked in anger
42 Alt. spelling
45 Jai ___
46 Duds
48 Opposite WSW
49 "Slow down!"
51 Ban rival
53 African language
54 "Relax, soldier!"
55 Makes, as a salary
57 Müeslix alternative
60 "The final frontier"
61 Meadowlands pace
62 ___ fixe (obsession)
63 Belief
64 Trig function
65 Boys

DOWN

1 Deep in thought
2 Goes by, as time
3 Put in place
4 Prefix with -hedron
5 Jail cell parts
6 Vase
7 Maiden name preceder
8 Activity with chops and kicks
9 Early fur trader John Jacob ___
10 Person using a library card
11 Less wordy
12 Stock page heading: Abbr.
13 "For shame!"
18 Rude
22 Brit. legislators
24 Semimonthly tide
25 Joins up
26 Rage
27 Lunar New Year
30 Tennis court call
34 Under
35 Pain in the neck
36 IOU
37 White wine cocktail
38 ___ Juan, P.R.
39 "Roll Over Beethoven" grp.
40 Healthful cereal grain
42 Front porch
43 Liqueur flavoring
44 Overnight flights
46 Back, at sea
47 Teases
50 Beginning
52 Lubricate again
54 Pot starter
55 N.Y.C. winter clock setting
56 King Kong, e.g.
58 Spoonbender Geller
59 Coal unit

by Sarah Keller

ACROSS

1 Round after the quarters
6 Sweetheart
10 Music staff symbol
14 Frank who directed "It's a Wonderful Life"
15 Noisy quarrels
16 Come-on
17 [ ]
20 Stranded motorist's need
21 Bump off
22 [ ]
28 Stridex target
29 Bank take-back, briefly
30 #1 Oak Ridge Boys hit
32 Swelling shrinker
35 Star's part
39 Nasdaq unit: Abbr.
40 [ ]
42 Bamboozle
43 Attack
45 Number on either side of a +
47 Time-honored
49 "Othello" villain
50 Paycheck abbr.
52 [ ]
55 Penetrated
57 Mattel card game
58 Answers to 17-, 22-, 40- and 52-Across, literally
65 Gofer: Abbr.
66 Letters
67 Bridal path
68 Flower fanciers
69 C & W mecca, with "the"
70 Band with the 1984 hit "Legs"

DOWN

1 "Nova" subj.
2 Grab a bite
3 AWOL trackers
4 Nest-egg investment, briefly
5 Sleigh driver
6 Look without buying
7 Geological span
8 Sense of wonder
9 Cold war initials
10 Amtrak amenity
11 Rest atop
12 Come after
13 Celebratory suffix
18 Hither's opposite
19 Watched over
22 Slap target, sometimes
23 "Wag the Dog" actress Anne
24 La Scala production
25 Corn holder
26 In sum
27 "Z" actor Montand
31 Paul Simon's "___ Rock"
33 First name of the second first lady
34 Chromosome constituent
36 Bounding main
37 Vowel sound in "phone" and "home"
38 Fund, as a university chair
41 Yours, in Ypres
44 Scams
46 "Hägar the Horrible" cartoonist Browne
48 In a gloomy way
50 Answer choice on a test
51 Employed
53 Austin-to-Dallas dir.
54 November birthstone
55 Wound protector
56 Jules Verne captain
59 Easy mark
60 Madam's mate
61 Designer Claiborne
62 Suffix with solo
63 "Strange Magic" grp.
64 Autumn mo.

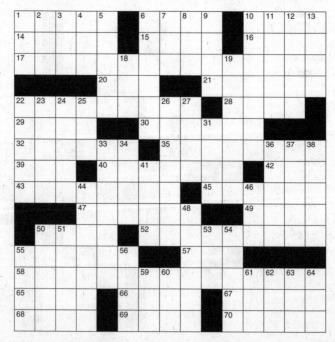

by Nancy Salomon

ACROSS

1 In years past
5 Throws on
9 Took steps
14 ___ of faith
15 Mirror-conscious
16 Halt
17 Supermarket section
18 "What ___?"
19 Film reviewers' showings
20 Shame a star of "Singin' in the Rain"?
23 Well-developed area?
24 Words said while holding hands
25 It may be brought out during a blackout
28 Israeli legislature
32 Netzero.com service
33 Radio's "___ & Anthony Show"
35 Corrida call
36 Pay no attention to a vampire?
40 Santa ___
41 Essential for an investigator
42 Sad sack
43 Softens
46 Rising stars
47 "Yes, ___!"
48 Rugby formation
50 Send a president out
55 Vanishes
56 Kind of horse
57 Actor Wyle
59 Gladiator's venue
60 Facility
61 Spoil, with "on"
62 Tripmeter feature
63 Tore
64 Brain part

DOWN

1 Antediluvian
2 Impecuniosity
3 Cartel city
4 Like a soap opera
5 Against, with "to"
6 ___ Lama
7 Some are slipped
8 Snick and ___
9 Give in
10 Big strings
11 Caboose, e.g.
12 Glimpse
13 ___ Plaines, Ill.
21 Big name in California wines
22 Former Pirates slugger Ralph
25 Chest material
26 Nitrogen compound
27 Sounding like one has a cold, say
28 N.B.A. star Jason
29 Lush
30 Aunt ___ of "Oklahoma!"
31 A sad thing to be in
33 Wallet fillers
34 School grp.
37 Prefix with sound
38 Not silently
39 Is in charge
44 Ancient ascetic
45 Barely catches, as the heels
46 Stretched in order to see
48 Deep-six
49 Selected
50 Bell the cat
51 Fateful date
52 Lashes
53 ___ court, law student's exercise
54 Make full
55 Distant
58 Bottom line?

by Sheldon Benardo

ACROSS

1 Martini garnish
6 Mrs. Dithers in "Blondie"
10 Colonel or captain
14 1976 Olympic gymnastics gold medalist ___ Comaneci
15 Assert
16 Away from the wind
17 OVALS
20 Word before roll or whim
21 Murder
22 "You're ___ talk!"
23 Affix one's John Hancock
24 On one's rocker?
26 K
32 Ship's crane
33 Needle parts
34 Évian, par exemple
35 Pizazz
36 Jazz instruments
38 ___ Strauss jeans
39 Be sick
40 Elisabeth of "Leaving Las Vegas"
41 Add a lane to, perhaps
42 STORY
46 "Lovely" Beatles girl
47 Bad news for a dieter
48 Assassinated
51 Atlantic Coast area, with "the"
52 Thrilla in Manila victor
55 X
59 Reverse, as an action

60 Commedia dell'___
61 Fit for a king
62 Gripe
63 Many a teenager's room
64 Alibi

DOWN

1 Aware of
2 Croquet area
3 Conception
4 Beaujolais, e.g.
5 Grovel
6 Checking out, as a joint
7 Kitchen hot spot
8 Gun, as an engine
9 "___ you kidding?"

10 Gilda of the early "S.N.L."
11 Soothing agent
12 Brilliantly colored salamander
13 Gambling game with numbers
18 Indian mystic
19 They're taboo
23 "Wheel of Fortune" turn
24 Eye sore
25 11's in blackjack
26 Actress Shire
27 Picture frames lacking corners
28 Under a spell
29 Must-haves
30 Icicle holders
31 Destroy
32 It may be new, raw or big

36 Gun blast
37 Mystique
38 Circus animal with a tamer
40 Hogs
41 Novelists
43 Son of Poseidon
44 Playing marbles
45 Alternative to check or charge
48 Pond gunk
49 Jay of late-night
50 Wing ___ prayer
51 Young 12-Downs
52 Jason's ship
53 Fibber
54 Without doing anything
56 Ewe's mate
57 Mine find
58 "___ lost!"

by Mark T. Milhet

ACROSS

1 It may be played in elevators
6 MGM co-founder
10 Soldier who's nowhere to be found
14 Entree served with a ladle
15 Pro's opposite
16 Waiter's offering
17 Psychologist sweethearts?
19 Sea dog
20 These can be vital
21 "___ Angel" (1960 #1 hit)
23 Deli loaf
24 Manila ___
25 Ring of frangipani blossoms
27 Lender terms: Abbr.
29 How a psychologist might start over?
34 Mustard city
37 Sleigh pullers
38 10 C-notes
39 Anthem with both English and French lyrics
41 Preordain
43 Manage without assistance
44 Jacob's twin
46 Hosiery brand
47 Psychologist's fast-food order?
50 Grope
51 Actor Stephen
52 "Now I see!"
55 ___, amas, amat . . .
57 The Tower of London was one
59 "Laughing" animals
62 Atticful

64 What a psychologist does at midnight in a motel pool?
66 Helper
67 Compos mentis
68 Struck forcefully
69 Kind of vision
70 Spotted
71 San Rafael's county

DOWN

1 Not the most rewarding work
2 Communications officer on "Star Trek"
3 Sharply piquant
4 Pond organism
5 Glazier's oven
6 W.C.
7 Erstwhile
8 "To be," in Tours
9 Smart aleck
10 Wake-up times, for short
11 Gets tiresome
12 Sole
13 Accompaniment for a madrigal
18 1952 Olympics site
22 "Morning Edition" airer
26 Punctuation used for stress
28 Wicker material
29 Melted-cheese dish
30 Genetic strand
31 Win over
32 New Year's Eve party hat, essentially
33 Shades
34 Remove, as a hat
35 Cake decorator
36 Best-selling "Workout" video maker

40 Far from elite
42 H. Rider Haggard novel
45 American or Swiss
48 M.D., e.g.
49 E. J. ___ Jr., longtime writer for The New Yorker
52 Choice words
53 Half of Hispaniola
54 Poplar tree
55 "Cleans like a white tornado" brand
56 1960's TV's "The Ghost and Mrs. ___"
58 "Fine by me"
60 Polite response from a ranch hand
61 Humorist Bombeck
63 Critical
65 Composer Rorem

by David Sullivan

ACROSS

1 Composer Satie
5 Progeny
10 Doorway part
14 Math sets
15 Sure-footed mountain animal
16 Village Voice award
17 Record label with many collections
18 Actor Paul of "American Graffiti"
19 Proceed
20 *Disney's ___ McDuck
22 *Mr. Television
24 Muffed
27 ___ vez (again): Sp.
30 Manfred Mann's "___ La La"
31 Ex of the Donald
36 Plot
38 Like
40 Elvis ___ Presley
41 Hit 1960's TV show with a hint to the nine starred clues in this puzzle
44 Karachi tongue
45 Actress Dolores ___ Rio
46 All the same
47 Monster
49 Journey part
51 Is profitable
52 Mount ___ (oldest of the Seven Sisters)
55 *"Highly charged" character on "The Addams Family"
59 *Gentleman rabbit of children's lit
64 Melville novel
65 Hubbub
68 "Got Milk?" ad partner
69 John Lennon's "Happy ___ (War Is Over)"
70 Explanatory phrase
71 Anorexic
72 Gabs
73 Camp sights
74 "___ Thin Air" (1997 best seller)

DOWN

1 Colorado Rockies game?
2 Campus program, initially
3 Hockey skater, informally
4 Smuggler's amount
5 Volunteer's offer
6 Cold showers?
7 *Man in a star-spangled suit
8 Thurman of "Pulp Fiction"
9 Wonderland cake words
10 It may get a nip on "Nip/Tuck"
11 Help in crime
12 Smaller than compact
13 "Adam ___"
21 Senator who wrote "Dreams From My Father"
23 Uganda's Amin
25 *"My Three Sons" housekeeper
26 Nimbus
27 Earth tone
28 Silents star Bara
29 *Brer Rabbit tale teller
32 *Chekhov title character
33 Cockroach of literature
34 Some court pleas, slangily
35 From the start
36 It's ripped off at the movies
37 Close
39 Docs' org.
42 Hew
43 Let float, as a currency
48 Café alternative
50 1940 Marx Brothers movie
53 Elliptical path
54 Highland attire
55 Cunning
56 Madame Bovary
57 Good, long bath
58 Turn's partner
60 Asian desert
61 Flattener
62 Fast time?
63 It can go around the world
66 Drink suffix
67 *Onetime Texas rice grower of note

by John Farmer

ACROSS

1 Madam's counterpart
4 Resort island near Venice
8 Voodoo charms
13 Poem of praise
14 Stove part
15 Inventor's goal
16 Slangy negative
17 Renowned bandleader at the Cotton Club
19 "I have an idea!"
20 Go before
21 Androids
23 By way of
24 24-hr. banking convenience
27 Dernier ___ (latest thing)
28 Raisin ___ (cereal)
30 Suffix with buck
31 Belief
33 Beats a hasty retreat
34 Emilia's husband, in "Othello"
35 Chinese province
36 They're "easy" to find in 17- and 53-Across and 3- and 24-Down
37 Rural's opposite
38 High: Prefix
39 Muskogee native
40 Walks like an expectant father
41 Noticed
42 Stoop
43 With 45-Across, for the time being
44 Mess up
45 See 43-Across
46 Monkeylike animals
49 Tends, as a patient

52 Butterfly catcher's tool
53 Seize power
56 Road goo
57 Reap
58 Arnaz of "I Love Lucy"
59 Hwy.
60 Dizzy-making drawings
61 Ooze
62 Big fat mouth

DOWN

1 Submarine-detecting system
2 Just 45 miles of it borders Canada
3 Place to get clean
4 When said three times, a real estate mantra
5 Several Russian czars
6 Bankruptcy cause
7 "___ upon a time . . ."
8 Island country south of Sicily
9 15-Down tribe
10 Synagogue attender
11 Keep ___ short leash
12 Hog's home
15 Where the buffalo roamed
18 Like Calculus II
22 Confer holy orders on
24 Jordan or Iraq
25 Ancient Roman robes
26 Mars has two

28 Train stoppers
29 Apply, as cream
30 Military branch with planes
31 Pursue
32 12" stick
37 Mustache site
39 Fairy king, in Shakespeare
45 Silently understood
46 Not tied down
47 Rodeo rope
48 ___ throat
49 "Good buddy"
50 Regulations: Abbr.
51 Not tied down
53 Sporty Pontiac
54 Grandmaster Flash's music genre
55 Alias, for short

by Adam G. Perl

ACROSS

1 Cheese choice
6 It's no free ride
9 Gangster gals
14 Like a Hitchcock audience, typically
15 Grant opponent
16 Poet T. S. ___
17 Hitchhikers' needs
18 Turkish chief
19 Not completely white anymore
20 "Where did ___ wrong?"
21 Testing, as one's patience
24 S-shaped molding
25 Fear
27 Scant
29 Like 90 proof liquor
30 Non-Rx
31 Four Monopoly properties: Abbr.
34 European carrier
35 Bad winner's behavior
37 "Who's the ___?"
40 Peking or Siam suffix
41 Direction for a wagon train
42 Large turnip
45 ___ good clip
47 Valuable rock
48 Spying device
49 Reviewer
53 Outsiders may not get it
56 Put a new handle on
57 Ticklish muppet
59 Thick-skinned critters
61 33 1/3 r.p.m. spinners
62 Many a pope
64 Before, in poetry

65 California team [and 18 letters in the grid to circle . . . and then connect using three lines]
67 Lightly burn
68 N.Y.C. ave. between Park and Third
69 Red Square notable
70 Gang's slanguage
71 Allow
72 Newsboy's shout of old

DOWN

1 Comic page offerings
2 Scale reading
3 Not outside
4 Memphis-to-Mobile dir.
5 Troubadour's six-stanza verse

6 Pot composition
7 Sponsorship
8 Gardener's vine support
9 Dr.'s field
10 Stews
11 Common Valentine's Day gift
12 Theater section
13 Eye ailment
22 Lively piano pieces
23 Córdoba cat
26 ___ nova (1960's dance)
28 Zenith competitor
32 Surgical assts.
33 ___ Snorkel
35 Fed. purchasing org.
36 Wit who wrote "When in doubt, tell the truth"
37 Sis's sib
38 Your and my

39 Hot under the collar
40 Shade of white
43 U.K. radio and TV inits.
44 Violinist Leopold
45 Prefix with 25-Across
46 Railroad support
50 Skill
51 Damage
52 Business jet maker
54 Zaire, now
55 "Yes ___, Bob!"
57 She, in Roma
58 Bandit's refuge
60 Call in a bakery
63 Holiday in Vietnam
66 Bewitch

by Patrick Merrell

ACROSS

1 Nightclub light
5 Jorge's eight
9 Ace taker
14 Sailor's patron saint
15 Pearl Buck heroine
16 Beethoven's "___ Joy"
17 Penthouse feature
18 6-Down's subj.
19 Overseas assembly
20 Cowboy toppers
23 Sports facilities
24 Spills the beans
28 A Guthrie
30 Snookums
31 French/English conflict that started in 1337
36 Crime lab evidence
37 Home mortgage stats
38 Moviegoer's reprimand
39 A message may be left after it
40 "What a relief!"
41 Resort area on the U.S./Canada border
45 Annual carrier of toys
47 Push
48 Like George Carlin
51 Time for a 52-Down wake-up call?
55 Natalie Merchant's old group
57 Under
60 Chicago paper, for short
61 Raised
62 Christmas wish
63 Sight from Bern
64 Film director Petri
65 Noted 1999 hurricane
66 Flexible Flyer, for one
67 Aid and abet: Abbr.

DOWN

1 English-speaking Caribbean island
2 "Middlemarch" author
3 Watch word?
4 In these times
5 "Eet ees so nice!"
6 One of nine sisters in myth
7 Lacks
8 Words with go or cheap
9 Rude subway rider
10 Sight from the Black Sea
11 "Jeopardy!" supercontestant Jennings
12 In-flight info: Abbr.
13 Balderdash
21 Money with Garibaldi's picture
22 "Betsy's Wedding" star
25 Fifth Avenue spa
26 Like composition paper
27 Springs
29 Roughly
31 "No thanks!"
32 Seat of Marion County, Fla.
33 Census choice
34 Cinemax alternative: Abbr.
35 Taylor or Tyler
39 Uneasy feelings
41 "Oops!"
42 "What a mistake!"
43 Convertible
44 Reclined
46 Boneheadedness
49 Smidgens
50 Pinkish hue
52 See 51-Across
53 ___ the hole
54 PC program
56 Bog
57 Beach bottle letters
58 Daughter of Loki, in Norse myth
59 Altitudinous Ming

by Elizabeth C. Gorski

12 MONDAY

ACROSS

1 Healthful retreats
5 Cartoonist Thomas who attacked Boss Tweed
9 Sleeves cover them
13 Chair designer Charles
15 Addict
16 Outscore
17 "Ain't it the ___?!"
18 Computer info
19 River of Spain
20 Germfree armored vehicle?
23 Ruined
24 H, in Greece
25 Golf gadget
26 Jan. and Feb.
27 Bring forth
30 Looks lasciviously
32 It may be served à la mode
33 Motorist's org.
34 Order between "ready" and "fire"
35 Money for busting up monopolies?
41 Buck's mate
42 ___ Paulo, Brazil
43 Mentalist Geller
45 Peak
48 Reddish hair dye
50 Cambridge sch.
51 "For ___ a jolly . . ."
52 Mimic
54 Agree (to)
56 Vandalism or thievery?
60 Rung
61 Go no further
62 Embarrass
64 Sailors

65 Princes but not princesses
66 Frank ___, Al Capone lieutenant
67 Otherwise
68 Gaelic
69 Math subj. with angles

DOWN

1 Order between "ready" and "go"
2 "They're following me!" feeling
3 South Pole explorer Roald
4 Melee
5 Unclothed
6 Pronto, on memos
7 Couch
8 Blue eyes or dark hair, e.g.

9 Assist illegally
10 Money-back offer
11 George Eliot's "Silas ___"
12 Feeds, as a fire
14 Rise and ___
21 Tranquilize
22 Where L.A. and S.F. are
23 Caller of balls and strikes
28 Nasser's dream: Abbr.
29 Make happen
31 Bird more than five feet tall
34 Hard-to-hum
36 QB's scores
37 Bits
38 ___ Clemente
39 List from 1 to whatever

40 Toasts
44 Cousin ___ of "The Addams Family"
45 Modest
46 U-Haul truck, e.g.
47 Fragrant compounds
48 Victim of Achilles
49 Egyptian dam
53 Rapper's entourage
55 Edna Ferber novel
57 ___ dixit
58 Some Saturns
59 Cathedral recess
63 Her's partner

by Sheldon Benardo

ACROSS

1 Actor B. D. of "Law & Order: S.V.U."
5 Bridge maven Sharif
9 S.U.V. alternative, informally
14 Earth Day subj.
15 Yellow-striped ball in pool
16 One of the Astaires
17 Sewing case
18 Cereal choice
19 Paint ingredient
20 "We never had this conversation, O.K.?"
23 Former flier to J.F.K.
24 Abridges
25 "Vidi"
27 "Am I supposed to be impressed?"
30 Avoidance of reality
34 Inventor's cry
35 Truth, old-style
37 Son of Isaac
38 "Just mumbling"
42 "Rule, Britannia" composer
43 4:1, e.g.
44 Holiday celebrated in Little Saigon
45 Therapy session subjects
48 Dracula player
50 ___ II (razor)
51 ___ Wenner, founder of Rolling Stone
52 Middle O of O-O-O
54 Musical with the song "Shall We Dance?"
60 Bring down
62 See 49-Down
63 Promise
64 Bluffer's game
65 Marshes
66 Like the president's office
67 Boardroom V.I.P.'s
68 Tart plum
69 Basketball great Archibald

DOWN

1 Garden intruder
2 Eight: Prefix
3 Proper ___
4 Computer snag
5 Computer starter
6 Some Spanish Surrealist works
7 Gray's subj.
8 Philosopher Descartes
9 Solidarity leader Lech
10 Oklahoma city
11 Figures out
12 Cheers for el toro
13 What one at the head of a line likes to hear
21 Somewhat
22 Boom box port
26 Monkey's uncles?
27 Exorcist's target
28 Chicago air hub
29 Baked dessert with shelled ingredients
30 Singer James and others
31 Whiskey order
32 After-Christmas events
33 Civilian clothes
36 Meanie
39 Deborah of 54-Across
40 Pasta style
41 Children
46 Many John Wayne flicks
47 P.T.A. meeting venue: Abbr.
49 Chew, as a 62-Across
51 Ultrapatriot
52 Gift-wrapping need
53 "Life is like ___ of chocolates"
55 Flows back
56 Marlboro competitor
57 Astronomical sighting
58 "Shoot!"
59 Nothing doing?
61 Wall St. regulator

by Elizabeth C. Gorski

ACROSS

1 Large 40-Across of people
5 & 9 40-Across seen in parentheses
14 Big lot
15 Chest part
16 Tourist draw
17 Stadium near La Guardia
18 Succulent plant
19 Swimming mammal
20 Start of a quip
23 Sensory input
24 Go over lines again
28 Amazed
31 E-mailer's button
34 Feminine suffix
35 Victor at Trafalgar, 1805
37 Daisy ___
38 Tail motions
39 Not a starter
40 Middle of the quip
43 Miss Piggy, to herself
44 Hearing-related
46 Bearded prez, informally
47 Some blacksmiths
49 Cartoon hyena
50 Pusher's nemesis
52 Black key
53 Racy
55 Norwegian saint
57 End of the quip
63 "___ español?"
66 Toward one side of a ship
67 Deco designer
68 Under way
69 Liven (up)
70 It's off the coast of Spain
71 & 72 Vaudevillian 40-Across
73 Certain 40-Across column

DOWN

1 Prepare potatoes, in a way
2 Dos cubed
3 Suds
4 Manatees
5 Southwest mission
6 School desk items
7 Plenty, old-style
8 Wrinkle or gray hair producer
9 Witch
10 No longer fit into
11 Telegraphed sound
12 Adelaide-to-Brisbane dir.
13 Red letters?
21 Ancient Greek theater
22 They may be marching
25 White coating
26 Sweater material
27 End
28 Low-level supporter?
29 Spay
30 Red-eyed one
32 Glowing piece
33 Scot's denial
36 Shading
41 Wharton grad
42 Cut
45 Now-computerized library feature
48 Quirky
51 Not apparent
54 Steaming
56 Scallionlike vegetables
58 Wine valley
59 Physics class subj.
60 Strongly advise
61 Phaser setting
62 Half of a vote
63 Is down with
64 Propeller's locale
65 Fancy neckwear

by Patrick Merrell

ACROSS

1 Opportunity to hit
6 Shoots 18, say
11 Rocks in a bar
14 Long green
15 The Beatles' "Eight Days ___"
16 Turf
17 Result of eating ice cream too fast, possibly
19 Moth-eaten
20 Best guess: Abbr.
21 Fastens with a band
22 "That is ___ . . ." (in other words)
24 Town next to Elizabeth, N.J.
26 Flexible, electrically
27 Fondue dip
32 Bops hard
35 Light as a feather
36 Pot's top
37 Spa wear
38 En ___ (all together)
40 Place for a ham
41 Where Schwarzenegger was born: Abbr.
42 "Lost our lease" event
43 Airplane seating option
44 Entreater's words
48 Asta's mistress
49 The whole ___ (everything)
53 Must, slangily
55 Debaters debate it
57 Shaq's alma mater: Abbr.
58 Copy
59 Sunshine State vacation area
62 Snore letter
63 3 on a par-5 hole, e.g.
64 Largish combo
65 Golfer Ernie
66 Collar inserts
67 Quaint footwear

DOWN

1 Color of waves of grain, in song
2 Sculpted figure
3 Bath toys
4 2001 role for Will Smith
5 Comb stoppers
6 Attic
7 Was in the red
8 Dregs
9 Shriner's topper
10 Missing many details
11 Kind of triangle
12 RC, for one
13 Whirling water
18 "___ 'er up!"
23 Pindar work
25 One-named supermodel
26 Plot unit
28 Studio prop
29 Insult, slangily
30 Spot for a warm pie
31 Falco of "The Sopranos"
32 Shawl or stole
33 Billing unit
34 Some voters
38 Yucatán native
39 Grand Paradiso, for one
40 Per ___
42 Attacks from the air
43 Sub sinkers, in slang
45 Young 'un
46 Catches sight of
47 Like gastric juice
50 Dementieva of tennis
51 So far
52 Corrodes
53 Stare intently
54 Kadett automaker
55 Fraternity party attire
56 Paris airport
60 Long. crosser
61 Keystone lawman

by Jim Hyres

ACROSS

1 "Hardball" channel
6 Tim of "WKRP"
10 Actor McGregor
14 Car hitch-up
15 Best of theater
16 Put on a scale
17 Mic check #1
20 Coverage co.
21 Gets across?
22 Like a sad sack
23 Long, long time
24 Within: Prefix
26 Mic check #2
31 Like hawks and auks
32 Words to an "old chap"
33 Genetic letters
36 Fix up
37 One of the Jacksons
39 Utah national park
40 A no. that's good when under 3.00
41 Laundromat loss, maybe
42 A beatnik may beat it
43 Mic check #3
47 Minister to
48 Carry on
49 Burger King or The Gap
52 Call after a toss
54 Toward the rear
57 Mic check #4
60 ___ Sea, east of the Ustyurt Plateau
61 Italian wine town
62 Latish bedtime
63 Puts on
64 40-Across, e.g.
65 Campus buys

DOWN

1 "How ___?"
2 Impostor
3 Prefix with second
4 Bull's urging
5 Draw near
6 Move, as a picture
7 Shangri-la
8 Sort of
9 Patriotic org.
10 Heretofore
11 Diminish
12 Straddling
13 Eye of ___ (witches' brew need)
18 Straddling
19 Thurber's fantasizer
23 Slightly
25 Straight, at the bar
26 Broken, in a way
27 Constantly
28 1967 war locale
29 Sounds from pens
30 Certain gasket
34 Scrapped, at NASA
35 Before long
37 Sportscaster Madden
38 Conclusive trial
39 Type of court defense
41 Court reporter
42 One in charge
44 Photos
45 Like dusk
46 Something seen with the Virgin Mary
49 Election hanger-on?
50 Sub
51 Actor Rickman
53 Prov. bordering Mont.
54 Michael J. Fox's role on "Family Ties"
55 Cyclist's problem
56 Some gobblers
58 Suffers from
59 Vane dir.

by Brendan Emmett Quigley

ACROSS

1 What a surfer rides
5 Do agricultural work
9 Pre-euro German money
14 Violinist Leopold
15 Side squared, for a square
16 When added up
17 Porn classification
19 AM/FM device
20 Rainbow's shape
21 Attractive
23 Nova ___
26 Battle exhortations
27 Followers of the Vatican
29 Dockworker's org.
30 Postponed
31 Driver entitled to free maps, perhaps
37 Sprinted
38 Grp. battling consumer fraud
39 Genetic letters
40 Big shoe request
44 Accumulate
46 Lumberjack's tool
47 Binds, as wounds
49 Sign-making aids
54 Gets the soap off
55 Part of a grand-father clock
56 "Then what . . . ?"
57 Handy ___ (good repairmen)
58 English king dur-ing the American Revolution
63 Feed, as a fire
64 Jazz's Fitzgerald
65 Horse color
66 Customs
67 Leave in, to a proofreader
68 At the ocean's bottom, as a ship

DOWN

1 Floor application
2 Secondary, as an outlet: Abbr.
3 Annoy
4 Inconsistent
5 Wealthy sort, slangily
6 ___ Ben Canaan of "Exodus"
7 Extend a subscription
8 ___ cum laude
9 Act of God
10 Horrid glances from Charles Grodin?
11 Hub projections
12 Kevin of "A Fish Called Wanda"
13 Wades (through)
18 Stand up
22 Bad, as a prognosis
23 Mold's origin
24 Something not really on Mars
25 Hypothesize
28 Kemo ___ (the Lone Ranger)
32 Pres. Lincoln
33 Help in crime
34 Button material
35 Follow
36 Metal filers
41 Beard named for a Flemish artist
42 Forgives
43 Astronaut Armstrong
44 Imitating
45 Darners
48 Mount where an ark parked
49 Charley horse, e.g.
50 ___-one (long odds)
51 Witch of ___
52 Olympic sleds
53 Refine, as metal
59 Bullring call
60 Debtor's note
61 Writer Fleming
62 It's kept in a pen

by Patrick Merrell

ACROSS

1 "___ as I can tell . . ."
6 Hurdles for future attorneys: Abbr.
11 Pudding fruit
14 Florida's Key ___
15 Florida's ___ Center
16 Form 1040 datum: Abbr.
17 Danish theologian (speller's nightmare #1)
19 Swe. neighbor
20 "As I Lay Dying" character
21 Afternoon: Sp.
22 What "nobody can" do, in song
23 Musical for which Liza Minnelli won a 1978 Tony
25 "___ it a shame"
27 German philosopher (speller's nightmare #2)
32 Walloped, old-style
35 Learning style
36 Cpl., for one
37 Astronomical ring
38 Pipe cleaner
40 20's touring cars
41 First daughter in the Carter White House
42 Certain Scandinavian
43 With regrets
44 Swedish statesman (speller's nightmare #3)
48 Locked (up)
49 Printing goofs
52 Romulus or Remus
54 City maps
57 Seldom seen
59 Colonial ___
60 Russian composer (speller's nightmare #4)
62 "Out of sight!"
63 Freak out
64 Navel variety
65 Brit. lawmakers
66 Reliance
67 Ceaselessly

DOWN

1 ___-Seltzer
2 Francis or Patrick, e.g.
3 Sassy
4 Accepts, as terms
5 Seoul soldier
6 Smooth, in music
7 Trade jabs
8 Military sch.
9 Railed against
10 The "S" in E.S.T.: Abbr.
11 Tweaked
12 Fe, to a chemist
13 Politico Hart
18 Design on metal
22 Cloning need
24 One-spot
26 "___-Devil"
28 Fraternity fun
29 Almost forever
30 Earth Day subj.
31 Pinkish
32 Head of old Iran
33 Papa's partner
34 Quadrennial events
38 Impoverished
39 T.L.C. givers
40 Speed reader?
42 Cheer leader?
43 Camera type, briefly
45 Game pieces
46 On-the-go group
47 Roughly
50 Spoonful, say
51 Alan of "The In-Laws"
52 Time in office
53 Trendy sandwich
55 Island party
56 Dangerous slitherers
58 Ogled
60 Nonunion workers: Abbr.
61 Pooh's pal

by Matt Skoczen

ACROSS
1 High-testing group
6 Drill locale: Abbr.
10 Frisbee, e.g.
14 Huffs and puffs
15 High-priced ticket request
16 ___ family, including bassoons and English horns
17 Very inclined
18 Director Kazan
19 Claimant's claim
20 Flirt's Valentine's gift?
23 Cry after a thoughtful silence
26 ___ the day
27 Enter cautiously
28 One illegally using a handicapped space?
32 Times Sq., e.g., in N.Y.C.
33 Beach Boy Wilson
34 Prospecting bonanzas
36 A dispiritingly large amount of e-mail
37 Extended families
39 ___ West of "Batman"
43 Pale with fright
45 Sticker figure
46 Massage locale
49 www.eyeglasses.com?
52 Crafty
54 Madeira Mrs.
55 "Get the picture?"
56 1960 Terry-Thomas movie (and title of this puzzle)
60 Embroidered ltr., often
61 "Whip It" rock group
62 Grayish
66 Stridex target
67 Sign
68 Wax removers
69 Clutter
70 Rumpelstiltskin's output
71 Flower part

DOWN
1 Mil. go-getters?
2 Proceed after grace
3 Wichita-to-Omaha dir.
4 Potpourri
5 Headache helper
6 Pub container
7 Cherry ___
8 Not fer
9 Maze features
10 Dim bulbs, so to speak
11 Graceful birds
12 "Amen!"
13 Small-plane maker
21 Sister
22 Croupier's tool
23 Getaway stoppers, briefly
24 Heavenly strings
25 "Dite alla giovine," e.g.
29 ___ sutra
30 Steak cut
31 Saturn model
35 Hindu wrap
37 Messy dish to eat
38 Spy novelist Deighton
40 Lodgings, informally
41 Tummy trouble
42 Parcel (out)
44 Neglected neighborhood
45 Things to mind
46 Dr. Seuss character
47 Frolic
48 Diet doctor
50 Donny or Marie
51 "Rin Tin Tin" TV night: Abbr.
53 Honors grandly
57 Verne captain
58 First name in daredevils
59 Toy with a tail
63 Chill
64 Univ. figure
65 Designer monogram

by Lee Glickstein and Nancy Salomon

ACROSS

1 Food lover's sense
6 Home for alligators
11 "Open ___ 9" (shop sign)
14 Pays to play poker
15 Talk show group
16 Early afternoon hour
17 "Pronto!"
19 Tribe related to the Hopi
20 Historic times
21 Use a hose on, as a garden
23 Rev. William who originated the phrase "a blushing crow"
27 "What so ___ we hailed . . ."
29 Singer Don of the Eagles
30 Opt for
31 Parking lot posting
32 Dahl who wrote "Charlie and the Chocolate Factory"
33 Subject of "worship"
36 Sound in a cave
37 Pocketbook
38 Ditty
39 Itsy-bitsy
40 Free-for-all
41 "I do" sayer
42 "Tom ___" (#1 Kingston Trio hit)
44 Smashed and grabbed
45 Adds up (to)
47 "___ keepers . . ."
48 Boxing matches
49 Skin soother
50 Sphere
51 "Pronto!"
58 Gibson who was People magazine's first Sexiest Man Alive
59 Hair-raising
60 Dickens's ___ Heep
61 "Later!"
62 Coral ridges
63 Shindig

DOWN

1 Bar bill
2 At ___ rate
3 Mudhole
4 Golf ball support
5 Ancient Jewish sect
6 Javelin
7 The "W" in V.F.W.
8 Plus
9 "Oh, give ___ home . . ."
10 Layered building material
11 "Pronto!"
12 Computer chip company
13 Suspicious
18 Card below a four
22 "The Sound of Music" setting: Abbr.
23 Nagging sort
24 Result of a treaty
25 "Pronto!"
26 Skillet lubricant
27 Moon stage
28 Part in a play
30 Actor Feldman
32 Contest specifications
34 Below
35 Requires
37 Hit with snowballs, say
38 Walked on
40 Loch Ness dweller, they say
41 Studies hard
43 Ump's call
44 Animal with a cub
45 Mushroom cloud maker
46 Amsterdam of "The Dick Van Dyke Show"
47 Goes by jet
49 "___ I care!"
52 Part of a giggle
53 Bad temper
54 ___ la la
55 Atmosphere
56 Turner who led a revolt
57 "___ will be done"

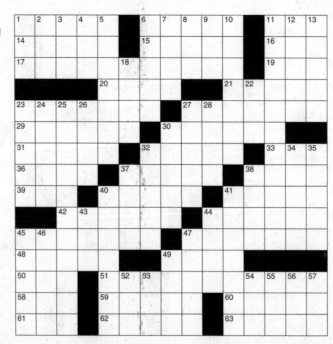

by Gregory E. Paul

ACROSS
1 Military bigwigs
6 Pad user
11 Gullible one
14 Consume
15 Luau serving
17 Wine bouquet
18 Consider, as a thought
19 Periodic arrival that causes much angst
21 Big times
22 Hardly a he-man
23 Member of a board of dirs.
24 Flower part
28 ___ Paulo
29 ___-all (score)
30 Really good joke
34 Seat at a wedding
37 What a 52-Across on a group of 19-Acrosses is
40 Whitney and others: Abbr.
41 Aim
42 Roman writer
43 Some Harvard grads: Abbr.
44 Certain Wall Street activities
46 Some are pale
48 La ___
51 Money guarantor, for short
52 Student's dream
57 "Hail, Stanford, Hail!," for one
59 Swashbuckling Flynn
60 Song from "No, No, Nanette"
61 Aptly named English novelist
62 Yearbook sect.
63 Kind of code at some schools
64 "The Sixth ___"

DOWN
1 Symbol on California's flag
2 Like a 52-Across
3 On
4 Clash of heavyweights
5 Spread out
6 Writer's guidelines
7 Turner and Louise
8 Diary bit
9 Penury
10 Sculler
11 Flat replacement
12 TV spy series starring Jennifer Garner
13 What stylophiles collect
16 Wing: Prefix
20 Equipment in kids' toy "telephones"
23 Prefix with legal
24 Dis
25 Perfectly
26 Gardner and others
27 ___ culpa
28 "Frasier" setting
31 Cereal grain
32 Actress Charlotte
33 Dodge City's home: Abbr.
34 Invoice stamp
35 House shader
36 Methods
38 Broadcasts
39 Like
43 Coffee for late at night
45 Go-carts
46 Grace ___ of "Will & Grace"
47 Certain beans
48 Tre + quattro
49 Ships' workers
50 Big dos
51 Saturated substances
52 Henry VIII's sixth
53 Place for a knot
54 Mother's mother, informally
55 Miniature sci-fi vehicles
56 Sheltered, at sea
58 Stylish, in the 60's

by Kevan Choset

ACROSS

1 "Poppycock!"
5 Iraqi port
10 Thompson of "Family"
14 Big name in oil
15 In-box contents
16 Wife, in legalese
17 Line to Penn Station
18 Sweater for the cold-blooded?
20 Cold-blooded idler?
22 TV extraterrestrial
23 Corrida cries
24 1983 Keaton title role
28 Microwave setting
30 Property receiver, in law
32 Latin 101 verb
33 Soaps, to soap operas, once
34 Cold-blooded dice roll?
38 Pit crew member
41 Salinger lass
45 Testified
46 English port
49 Tapir feature
50 Long, long time
51 Fictitious Richard
52 Cold-blooded children's play activity?
56 Cold-blooded fungi?
59 Samoan capital
60 Last of the Stuarts
61 Reason for a raise
62 Shape with a hammer

63 Stuff
64 Straws in the wind
65 Once, once

DOWN

1 Chaucerian verse form
2 1969 Mets victims
3 Napes
4 Gunpowder holder
5 Narcotic-yielding palms
6 Talisman
7 Calcutta wraps
8 Classic hotel name
9 ___ breve
10 Summer attire
11 Send packing
12 One of a Disney septet
13 Pairs holder?
19 Regal fur
21 Sticky stuff
25 Phone trigram
26 Key contraction?
27 ___ amis
29 Assume anew, as burdens
30 Barbary beast
31 Powell co-star in 1930's films
33 Jiffy
35 1598 edict city
36 "Wheel of Fortune" buy
37 A little butter?
38 Hosp. staffers
39 Velvet finish?
40 Navy noncom
42 Bass variety

43 Professors World Peace Academy group, informally
44 White-tie, say
46 Once-divided place
47 Homing pigeons' homes
48 Having one sharp
50 Prior to, in dialect
53 Air: Prefix
54 Feature of many a sympathy card
55 Get an eyeful
56 Put out
57 No longer divided
58 Collection suffix

by A. J. Santora

ACROSS

1 Big blowout
5 Vehicles with meters
9 Like some committees
14 Charles Lamb's nom de plume
15 Cookie with creme inside
16 Takes a card from the pile
17 Where to order egg salad
18 Flintstone fellow
19 Designer Karan
20 Practically gives away
23 Whole lot
24 Restless
27 Bandleader Shaw
29 Big galoots
31 "Vive le ___!"
32 Faint from rapture
33 Waterless
34 Mulligatawny, for one
35 Starts telling a different story
38 Theme park attraction
39 Bringing up the rear
40 Magician's rods
41 Gallery display
42 One who's suckered
43 Voting districts
44 Pushed snow aside
46 Saucy
47 Prepares to be punished
53 Desperately want
55 Homeboy's turf

56 Hurry up
57 Macho guys
58 English princess
59 River in an Agatha Christie title
60 Apply, as pressure
61 Not the original color
62 Meal in a pot

DOWN

1 People retire to these spots
2 Toward the sheltered side
3 Window feature
4 Dangerous bit of precipitation
5 Morning eyeopener

6 Turn signal
7 Brewski
8 Word after baking or club
9 Extras
10 Speak in a monotone
11 Loiter
12 Part of B.Y.O.B.
13 Jefferson Davis org.
21 David's weapon, in the Bible
22 Soft leather
25 Pings and dings
26 "Holy mackerel!"
27 Spinning
28 Celebrity's upward path
29 Cropped up
30 Pub offering

32 Throw out
33 "On the double!"
34 Bravura performances
36 Escape the detection of
37 Bunch of bees
42 Not half bad
43 Pulled dandelions, say
45 Be indecisive
46 Give a buzz
48 Certain herring
49 Chichi
50 Clubs or hearts
51 Capri, for one
52 Enjoy some gum
53 Friend of Fidel
54 Mystery author Stout

by Nancy Salomon and Kendall Twigg

ACROSS

1 "60 Minutes" airer
4 Gator relative
8 Nyasaland, now
14 Stephen of "The Crying Game"
15 Quad building
16 Readied for print
17 Post-O.R. stop
18 Meat marking
19 Brings disgrace to
20 Knowing no more than before
23 Part of a Vandyke
24 Mangy mutt
25 Stitch up
28 Lanchester of film
29 Words after a rude encounter, maybe
33 "___ extra cost!"
34 Devious sorts
35 One pointing, as a gun
39 Feel awful
41 Secret meeting
42 Mazola competitor
44 Gets a gander of
46 F.B.I.'s prime quarries
48 Twofold
52 Dr. who handles otitis cases: Abbr.
53 Neolithic ___
54 Where Idi Amin ruled
56 Buffet deal
59 Positive aspect
62 Swarming pest
63 Bio stat
64 Gawks
65 Low-cal
66 D.C. V.I.P.
67 Lecherous goat-men
68 Divorcés
69 Sink trap's shape

DOWN

1 Shrink in fear
2 Act nonchalant
3 Steamy spots
4 Water park slide
5 Most reckless
6 Shoppe sign word
7 Lobster portion
8 Snafus
9 Followers
10 Pants-on-fire guy
11 20's dispenser, for short
12 Teeny
13 Driver's lic. and others
21 Airport info: Abbr.
22 Convenience store bagful
25 Neuter
26 Part of B.P.O.E.
27 All-star game team, maybe
30 ___ roll (winning)
31 Like tasty cake
32 Anthem contraction
33 Metal joiner
35 Very top
36 Mineral in spinach
37 Atomizer's release
38 N.Y. winter setting
40 General in gray
43 Like a rowboat that's adrift
45 Teach
47 Dissenting vote
48 Vice president Quayle
49 Apprehension
50 Almanac sayings
51 Nears midnight
55 Billionaire Bill
56 Open-roofed
57 Leer at
58 Operating system on many Internet servers
59 ___ Constitution
60 Sch. group
61 Warmed the bench

by Nancy Kavanaugh

ACROSS

1 When doubled, a seafood entree
5 Is visibly frightened
10 Off one's trolley
14 "Yeah, right!"
15 Work ___
16 Pop's Brickell
17 Gigantic instrument?
19 "Take ___!" (track coach's order)
20 Holed up
21 First name in horror
22 Actress Sorvino
23 Instrument made in the lab?
27 Straits of ___
28 Tee follower?
29 Crew need
30 Set alight
33 Quattros, e.g.
37 Greet the day
39 Take your pick?
41 Federico of the Clinton cabinet
42 Touch up
44 Up
46 Early fifth-century year
47 First homeland security czar Ridge
49 Like some burgers
51 Instrument found at the Super Bowl?
56 Donald, to Dewey
57 Opposite of paleo-
58 Order of corn
59 "I'll be ___ of a gun!"
60 Missing instrument?
65 Ste. Jeanne ___
66 King of Thebes slain by Theseus
67 Inner: Prefix
68 January 1 song word
69 Surfer wannabe
70 Mail: Abbr.

DOWN

1 Shelley queen
2 "___ recall . . ."
3 Arrogant one's place
4 More uncertain
5 Chips' place
6 1955 merger grp.
7 Eric Clapton hit with a never-ending chorus
8 Flynn of "Captain Blood"
9 Dumpster emanation
10 Request to the Enterprise
11 Seat-of-the-pants performance
12 Papal wear
13 Calyx part
18 ___ one
23 Miner's filing
24 Binding exchanges
25 Magna ___
26 Roll-call call
27 "Watch out!"
31 P.C. part
32 When repeated, a cry of approval
34 U.S. citizen-to-be
35 The Dow, e.g.
36 Port ___ (Suez Canal city)
38 Door
40 1991 Grammy winner Cohn
43 Point
45 Keepsake
48 Good guy
50 Sanford of "The Jeffersons"
51 Thigh muscles
52 Take back
53 Squirrel's find
54 Old, but new again
55 Like unpopular umps
61 Mauna ___
62 Omega
63 Orch. section
64 Brillo rival

by Eric and Janinne Berlin

ACROSS

1 Musical genre pioneered by Bill Haley and His Comets
5 Cove
10 Partner of ready and willing
14 Unattractive tropical fruit
15 Voting site
16 Hit with the fist
17 Sunbather's award?
19 Sandwich fish
20 Still
21 Before, in poetry
22 Interpret without hearing
24 1051 on monuments
25 Edward who wrote "The Owl and the Pussycat"
26 Temples in the Far East
30 Assassinating
33 Oldtime actress Massey
34 Join, in woodworking
36 La Paz is its cap.
37 President after Tyler
38 Sun-bleached
39 "___ Ben Adhem," Leigh Hunt poem
40 Finish
41 Duelist Burr
42 Was bright, as the sun
43 Mark for misconduct
45 Gas ratings
47 Kuwaiti leader
48 Sun or planet
49 Depot baggage handlers
52 Actress Joanne
53 Next-to-last Greek letter
56 Wings: Lat.
57 Romantics' awards?
60 1/500 of the Indianapolis 500
61 Have a mad crush on
62 Colorful gem
63 [No bid]
64 Changed direction, as a ship
65 Actor Billy of "Titanic"

DOWN

1 Slippers' color in "The Wizard of Oz"
2 Shrek, for one
3 Blood problem
4 One of the same bloodline
5 Portugal and Spain together
6 Snout
7 Auction unit
8 List-ending abbr.
9 Tickled pink
10 Off course
11 Sad person's award?
12 Moon goddess
13 Old-time exclamation
18 Mrs. F. Scott Fitzgerald
23 Nectar source
24 Neurotic TV detective played by Tony Shalhoub
26 Spoke (up)
27 On one's own
28 Big recording artists' awards?
29 Brainy
30 Dictation taker
31 Nary a soul
32 Affixes (to)
35 Wedding 58-Down
38 Good sportsmanship
39 "Moby-Dick" captain
41 Song for a diva
42 Olympic gymnast Kerri
44 Roasts' hosts
46 ___ beef
49 Entrance to an expressway
50 Director Kazan
51 Scotch's partner
52 Dreadful
53 Insect stage
54 Go across
55 ___ of Man
58 See 35-Down
59 Family relation, for short

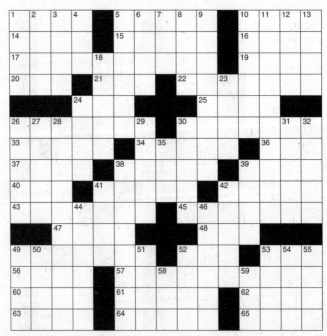

by Bernice Gordon

ACROSS

1 "If it ___ broke . . ."
5 "Guilty," e.g.
9 Clio winner
14 Most stuck-up
16 Poker ploy
17 "M.T.A." singers, 1959
19 Makes merry
20 Chart shape
21 "Bearded" flower
22 Mall binge
25 Murals and such
28 Dover's state: Abbr.
29 Rang out
31 Like gastric juice
32 40 winks
33 Group values
34 Paul Scott chronicles set in India
37 Weather map area
38 Have more troops than
39 Right on the map
40 Response to someone pointing
41 Actress Peeples
44 Take a gander at
45 Make ___ of (botch)
46 U.S.M.C. V.I.P.'s
47 German article
48 Is fearful of
50 Schubert chamber work
56 Fritter away
57 Unusual sort
58 Place for a kiss
59 Hatchling's home
60 Wagnerian earth goddess

DOWN

1 ___ Lindgren, Pippi Longstocking's creator
2 Naturally belong
3 It may be seen, heard or spoken, in a saying
4 Quick puffs
5 A.T.M. necessities
6 Trouser part
7 Pothook shape
8 J.D. holder: Abbr.
9 Golfer Palmer, to pals
10 See socially
11 Former Russian orbiter
12 "___ was saying . . ."
13 Prefix with natal
15 Up to, for short
18 Newspaper page
22 Home of the N.H.L.'s Sharks
23 Awards to be hung
24 Positions of esteem
25 Need liniment
26 Knee-slapper
27 Six-pointers, in brief
29 Hair-splitter?
30 LAX abbr.
31 Envelope abbr.
32 Gumball cost, once
33 The "E" in Q.E.D.
34 Cafeteria carrier
35 Vacuum feature
36 Buddy in Bordeaux
37 Lab charge
40 Mae West's "___ Angel"
41 Less cluttered
42 "You're so right!"
43 Courtroom fig.
45 Broadcaster
46 Sci-fi, for one
47 James of blues
48 The Everly Brothers, e.g.
49 Josh
50 Onetime Pan Am rival
51 Linden of "Barney Miller"
52 Body shop fig.
53 Java container
54 ___ kwon do
55 Football game divs.

by Len Elliott

ACROSS

1 White House affair, maybe
5 Beyond's partner
10 Part of Latin 101 conjugation
14 ___ Bator
15 Measure from the elbow to the end of the middle finger
16 Results may do this
17 With 33-, 36- and 40-Across, American born 7/28/1929
19 Press
20 Hip bone
21 Vital
22 Actress Hayek
23 Boating mishap
24 Neighbor of a Vietnamese
26 Period of time
28 Gary's home: Abbr.
31 Periods of time
32 Off
33 See 17-Across
35 Hall of Fame QB Dawson
36 See 17-Across
37 Name that's an alphabet trio
40 See 17-Across
41 Modern medical grps.
42 Composer/ writer Ned
44 Cable inits.
45 Ages and ages
46 Most blue
48 ___-mo
49 Right hands
50 New Deal inits.
53 Celebrity photographer Herb
56 Where D.D.E. went to sch.

57 Topper made popular by 17- and 36-Across
59 Retro phone feature
60 Laughing gas, for one
61 "Born Free" lioness
62 Lodges
63 Baseball datum
64 Part of CBS: Abbr.

DOWN

1 Kodak competitor
2 Mideast carrier
3 Reserved
4 Commission's task
5 Top-notch
6 Mail may be sent in this
7 Award for Tony Kushner
8 Like old records
9 Summer on the Seine
10 Wilbur or Orville Wright
11 Florida player
12 Bouquets
13 "Seduced" senator of film
18 Man in black?
22 Cry on a hog farm
25 During
26 "2001" mainframe
27 See red?
28 Structural members
29 Votes in Versailles
30 Kirsten of "Spider-Man"
34 Marble feature
36 Genuflection points
37 Without a hitch
38 Proverbial brickload

39 Seagoing letters
40 Trials
41 DNA structures
42 Granola ingredient
43 One who's "out"
46 Any of the Fahd ruling family
47 ___ 12 and 20
48 Angel's favorite letters
51 Dancer's exercise
52 13-Down player
54 Itar-___ news agency
55 E.R. order
57 Med. test result
58 ___ canto

by Mark Elliot Skolsky

ACROSS
1 Mall component
6 Genesis twin
10 Fly like an eagle
14 Hiker's path
15 Goatee's locale
16 Time for eggnog
17 Having no entryways?
19 A.A.A. recommendations: Abbr.
20 Left on a map
21 How some ham sandwiches are made
22 Letter after theta
23 Disney World attraction
25 Opposite of whole, milkwise
27 "French" dog
30 "I'm ready to leave"
32 Down Under bird
33 Britannica, for one: Abbr.
35 "Thanks, Pierre!"
38 Squeal (on)
39 ___ standstill (motionless)
40 City that Fred Astaire was "flying down to" in a 1934 hit
42 "Dear old" family member
43 Jogs
45 Looks sullen
47 Poetic palindrome
48 Tributary
50 Word before Nevada or Leone
52 Hold back
54 Give a benediction to
56 Ball field covering
57 Motionless
59 Campaign funders, for short
63 Buffalo's lake
64 Having no vision?
66 Submarine danger

67 Number between dos and cuatro
68 Weird
69 Habitual tipplers
70 Gumbo vegetable
71 Modify to particular conditions

DOWN
1 Put in the hold
2 "___ Grit" (John Wayne film)
3 Quaker ___
4 Ran amok
5 Santa's little helper
6 Commercial prefix with Lodge
7 In a moment
8 Bright and breezy
9 Still in the out-box, as mail
10 Injection selection
11 Having no commandment?

12 Prince Valiant's wife
13 Plopped down again
18 Museum guide
24 Delighted
26 Gradual absorption method
27 Saucy
28 Bradley or Sharif
29 Having no typeset letters?
31 Stocking shade
34 Where to watch whales in Massachusetts, with "the"
36 Writer John Dickson ___
37 Inkling
41 "The only thing we have to fear is fear ___": F.D.R.
44 Prairie homes

46 It goes around the world
49 Mississippi River explorer
51 Caught sight of
52 Agenda details
53 The first part missing in the author's name ___ Vargas ___
55 The second part missing in the author's name ___ Vargas ___
58 Istanbul resident
60 Taj Mahal locale
61 Intel product
62 Typesetting mark
65 Poseidon's domain

by Holden Baker

ACROSS

1 Sir, in India
6 Gounod production
11 Word with toll or roll
14 ___ acid
15 Cartoonist Kelly and others
16 Singer on half the 1984 album "Milk and Honey"
17 Hard-to-please labor protester?
19 Bird's beak
20 ¢¢¢
21 Unc's wife
23 Busta Rhymes rhymes
27 Like some of the Sahara
28 Flies off the handle
29 West Indian native
30 Mar. 17 figure, from 58-Across
31 Hooch
33 Punch in the stomach response
36 Shirts and blouses
37 Beetle Bailey's commander
38 ___'acte (intermission)
39 With 4-Down, modern printing fluid
40 Farm fence features
41 Prefix with -gon
42 A paramedic may look for one
44 Employ
45 Popular Ford
47 Skilled in reasoning
49 Eve's downfall
50 Lose at the bank?
51 Race unit
52 Cheap promotional trip?
58 See 30-Across

59 1973 #1 Rolling Stones hit
60 Bench site
61 Long-distance letters
62 Sailors' stories
63 Like a beach

DOWN

1 Doofus
2 Parisian pal
3 Drunk's utterance
4 See 39-Across
5 Political protest of sorts
6 Because of, with "to"
7 Successful negotiation results
8 The "E" of B.P.O.E.
9 Way to go: Abbr.

10 "Steps in Time" autobiographer
11 Pretty woman's hat?
12 Singer Bryant
13 ___ Smith, first female jockey to win a major race
18 Cross and Parker products
22 Where: Lat.
23 Musical breaks
24 ___-Detoo ("Star Wars" droid)
25 Plaything that yips?
26 Vacation spots
27 Loll
29 Gear teeth
31 Au naturel
32 Globe
34 Holy Roman emperor, 962-73
35 Swiss money

37 Talk back
38 Creepy: Var.
40 Toronto ballplayer
41 Multicar accidents
43 www.yahoo.com, e.g.
44 Pilgrimage to Mecca
45 Actress Shire
46 Besides, with "from"
47 Actor Alan
48 "The Highwayman" poet Alfred
50 Bridge builder, e.g.: Abbr.
53 Italian article
54 Actress Vardalos
55 "The Wizard of Oz" locale: Abbr.
56 Bitter ___
57 Slinky or boomerang

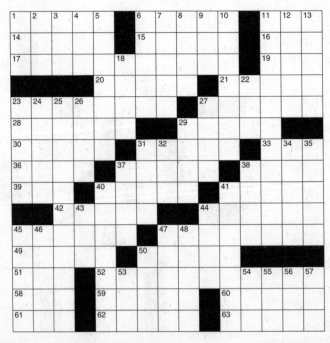

by Roy Leban

ACROSS
1 Variety of guitar
6 Walked (on)
10 Touches with a live wire
14 Volcanic creation
15 Part to play
16 Jacques's steady
17 Make smooth
18 Crude org.
19 Mushroom cap part
20 Hand raiser's declaration
23 ___ de guerre
24 Far from haute cuisine
25 1945 John Wayne western
27 Hand raiser's shout
32 The Louisville Lip
33 Freedom from hardship
37 "Tell Laura ___ Her" (1960 hit)
40 Burrowing insect
41 "I mean it!"
42 Leeway
44 Not healthy
45 Hand raiser's cry
50 Fountain basin feature
53 Violinist Leopold
54 Yes, to 16-Across
55 Hand raiser's request
61 Girl in Lou Bega's "Mambo No. 5"
63 "Dies ___"
64 Confident way to solve crosswords
65 Not completely closed
66 "Don't look at me!"
67 Griffin of the N.B.A.

68 Bird that "at heaven's gate sings," in Shakespeare
69 Within the hour
70 Rough tools

DOWN
1 Stock market turns
2 Parliament city
3 Not piquant
4 Take back
5 Opera with "Ave Maria"
6 ___ l'oeil
7 Part of a climber's gear
8 Couturier Cassini
9 Figures out
10 Quick sidestep
11 Protein acid
12 Person who sits in front of a cabin
13 City famously visited by Martin Luther King, Jr. in 1965
21 Motion picture angle: Abbr.
22 "Beyond the Sea" singer, 1960
26 Numbers game
27 Banshee's cry
28 "___ Enchanted" (2004 film)
29 Gasser
30 Ask for more issues
31 Beaver, e.g.
34 "Dream Children" essayist
35 Threshold
36 Peddle
38 Short biography

39 Body of good conduct
40 Hurry-scurry
43 Waifs
46 Adopt, as a pet
47 March sound
48 Harder to grasp
49 "Beverly Hills 90210" girl
50 Fable conclusion
51 Board used in "The Exorcist"
52 It was played by George Harrison
56 Suffix with sock
57 Denouncer of Caesar, 63 B.C.
58 Supports
59 Use scissors
60 Squeezes (out)
62 Torah holder

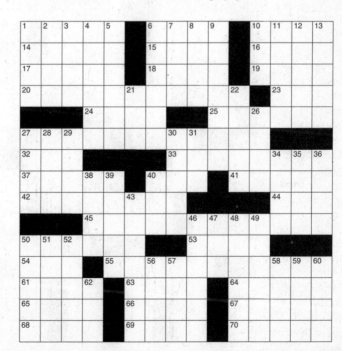

by Raymond Hamel

ACROSS
1 Pitches four balls to
6 Cain's brother
10 Insurrectionist Turner and others
14 Not reacting chemically
15 Muse of history
16 Monogram part: Abbr.
17 Pilfer
18 Kitchen gadget that turns
20 "Faster!"
22 No great ___
23 Iced tea flavoring
26 Full complement of fingers
27 Sob
30 Before, in poetry
31 Classic gas brand
34 Composer Rachmaninoff
36 Midsection muscles, for short
37 "Faster!"
40 Knight's title
41 Rat or squirrel
42 Dye containers
43 Western Indian
44 Linear, for short
45 Rope-a-dope boxer
47 Fixes
49 1960's–70's space program
52 "Faster!"
57 Cramped space
59 Rich cake
60 Primer dog
61 Sharif of film
62 Gives an audience to

63 Band with the 1988 #1 hit "Need You Tonight"
64 Monthly payment
65 Birds by sea cliffs

DOWN
1 Bit of smoke
2 Contrarians
3 Bloodsucker
4 Volcano that famously erupted in 1883
5 Acts of the Apostles writer
6 Bank holdings: Abbr.
7 Dull
8 Mozart's "a"
9 Circle
10 Daughter of a sister, perhaps
11 Ben Stiller's mother
12 Bit of business attire
13 Narrow water passage: Abbr.
19 Washed-out
21 Money for retirement
24 What a satellite may be in
25 Digs with twigs?
27 Kennel club info
28 "Son of ___!"
29 Had a cow
31 ___ salts
32 Luxury hotel accommodations
33 Safe

35 Mahler's "Das Lied von der ___"
38 Snowman of song
39 Villain
46 Can't stand
48 Amounts in red numbers
49 Notify
50 Ship's navigation system
51 Weird
53 Norse thunder god
54 Terse directive to a chauffeur
55 Panache
56 "___ of the D'Urbervilles"
57 Popular TV police drama
58 WB competitor

by M. Francis Vuolo

ACROSS

1 Home to Honolulu
5 Sticky stuff
9 Mends, as socks
14 "The Good Earth" mother
15 Good lot size
16 "The Waste Land" poet
17 Where to find a hammer, anvil and stirrup
19 Oro y ___ (Montana's motto)
20 Charlie Rose's network
21 An Arkin
22 Ease up
23 It may be found in front of a saloon
26 Tone-___ (rapper)
27 Strong hand cleaner
31 "Doe, ___ . . ." ("The Sound of Music" lyric)
34 Queens stadium
36 6 on a phone
37 Picture-filled item often seen in a living room
41 "C'___ la vie"
42 Missing the deadline
43 Bonkers
44 Hopelessness
47 What 20-Across lacks
48 Foyer
54 Former White House pooch
57 Private eyes
58 Romance
59 Seed coverings
60 International business mantra
62 Carnival show
63 Lends a hand
64 Valuable rocks
65 Odist to a nightingale
66 McCartney played it in the Beatles
67 Top ratings

DOWN

1 That certain "something"
2 It may be airtight
3 Verb with thou
4 Sturm ___ Drang
5 Irish dialect
6 Continental divide?
7 Big ape
8 ___ capita
9 Unseat
10 Apportions
11 Inlets
12 Post-it
13 Ollie's partner in old comedy
18 Capital of Punjab province
22 Faithful
24 Staff leader?
25 First-year West Pointer
28 Melville romance
29 Before long
30 Snaillike
31 Passed with flying colors
32 Teaspoonful, maybe
33 Young newts
34 Football legend Bart
35 Where a rabbit may be hidden
38 10-point type
39 First-born
40 Twaddle
45 Small shot
46 Liqueur flavorers
47 Admission
49 Courtyards
50 Must-haves
51 Vigilant
52 Waterproof wool used for coats
53 Silt deposit
54 Word that can follow the end of 17-, 23-, 37-, 48- or 60-Across
55 "Dies ___" (liturgical poem)
56 Old Italian coin
60 Groovy
61 Twaddle

by Sarah Keller

ACROSS

1 Govt. agency since 1949
4 They may be sordid
9 Early associate of Freud
14 Popular Quaker cereal
15 Eight-ish?
16 Sporty Japanese car
17 Marceau character
18 See 33-Across
19 Intimidate, with "out"
20 Lovable curmudgeon of 1970's TV
23 Excitement
24 Treetop nibbler
28 Brownstone front
32 Play the peeping Tom
33 With 18-Across, capital of the United Arab Emirates
36 Mustang site
38 A Turner
39 Noted rehab facility
43 End in ___
44 Bucks
45 Winter Chi. clock setting
46 Lassie, for one
49 Close-knit group
51 Patella
53 Majestic
57 "The Blue Dahlia" star
61 Wing it
64 Lose one's mind
65 Loire valley product
66 Something thrown for a loop?

67 Atlantic Ten school home
68 Ike's command, once: Abbr.
69 The Dow, e.g.
70 More sound
71 Easygoing

DOWN

1 Spoil
2 Prepare eggs in a way
3 Stray place: Abbr.
4 Sole-searching, maybe?
5 Suffer
6 Shot
7 No-no: Var.
8 Armrest?
9 Current measure
10 British P.M. before Gladstone

11 Put in position
12 List ender
13 Fan noise
21 Pinafore letters
22 Laotian money
25 Swiss capital
26 Conclusion
27 Formally approve
29 Gut reaction?
30 Blue Moon of baseball
31 Contender of 1992 and 1996
33 One way to be taken
34 Be assured of
35 Handy
37 Scent
40 Air
41 Mid second-century year

42 Home of Goose Bay
47 Solitary confinement cell, in slang
48 Ring locale
50 Slithery swimmer
52 Bounces on a stick
54 Court instrument
55 Japanese dog
56 Tanglewood site, in Massachusetts
58 One of Asta's owners
59 "___ the case"
60 Nursing home staff?
61 Clay, now
62 Rather in the news
63 Cause of many trips, once

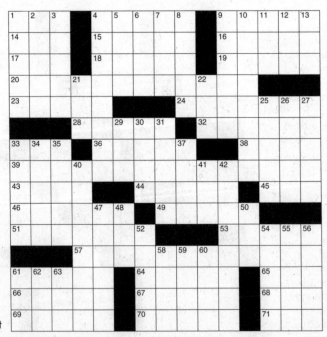

by Alan Arbesfeld

ACROSS

1 Poi source
5 "The Thin Man" dog
9 Rum-soaked cakes
14 Stench
15 Where an honoree may sit
16 Friend, south of the border
17 Rocket scientist's employer
18 Prefix with potent
19 Alpine song
20 Not much
23 ___ glance (quickly)
24 Center of activity
25 Grammys, e.g.
29 Tip for a ballerina
31 Aide: Abbr.
35 Funnel-shaped
36 Craze
38 Hurry
39 Activities that generate no money
42 Surgery spots, for short
43 Indians of New York
44 Jack who ate no fat
45 Seeded loaves
47 Dog-tag wearers, briefly
48 Choirs may stand on them
49 Overly
51 Loser to D.D.E. twice
52 Boatswains, e.g.
59 R-rated, say
61 Poker payment
62 Confess
63 Tutu material
64 Rude look
65 Peru's capital
66 Back tooth
67 Slips
68 Fizzless, as a soft drink

DOWN

1 Cargo weights
2 Sandler of "Big Daddy"
3 Painter Bonheur
4 Face-to-face exam
5 Takes as one's own
6 Pago-Pago's land
7 Salon application
8 Where Nepal is
9 Louisiana waterway
10 Microscopic organism
11 Bridge declarations
12 Questionnaire datum
13 Note after fa
21 Scottish beau
22 "A League of ___ Own" (1992 comedy)
25 Cast member
26 "What, me ___?"
27 Liqueur flavorer
28 Speed (up)
29 Blackmailer's evidence
30 Burden
32 English county
33 Ravi Shankar's instrument
34 Checkups
36 1052, in a proclamation
37 St. Francis' birthplace
40 Lingo
41 Raises
46 "A Streetcar Named Desire" woman
48 Directs (to)
50 Stream bank cavorter
51 "___ you" ("You go first")
52 Clout
53 Connecticut campus
54 Unique individual
55 Ranch newborn
56 Diabolical
57 Capital south of Venezia
58 Whack
59 Bank amenity, for short
60 Pair

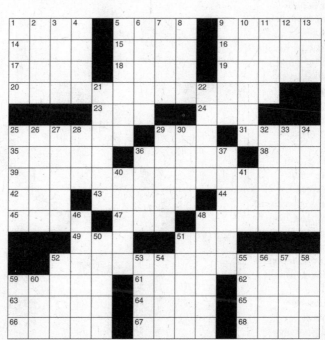

by Joy C. Frank

ACROSS

1. ___ the Red
5. Fragrant blossom
10. "Right on!"
14. Woodworking groove
15. Excitedly
16. Stack
17. He wrote "Utopia" in an ancient language
19. Yard sale tag
20. Partner of "ifs" and "ands"
21. Arterial trunks
23. Do a favor
26. Be charitable
28. Tilted
29. Oxidize
30. A.A.A. suggestion: Abbr.
33. Office stamp
34. Better halves
35. Disney Store item
36. "How Sweet ___"
37. Mocks
38. Something that shouldn't be left hanging
39. Twilight time to a poet
40. More immense
41. Rear
42. TV prog. with a different host each week
43. Cupid's counterpart
44. Author Lee
45. Inner circle member
47. Keats and others
48. Hogan dweller
50. Seed cover
51. Oscar winner Guinness
52. Blind poet who often wrote in an ancient language
58. Desertlike
59. Gladden
60. Dust Bowl refugee
61. Pianist Dame Myra
62. Dravidian language
63. ___ contendere

DOWN

1. Summer hrs. in N.J.
2. Cheer
3. Life-changing statement
4. Farm vehicles
5. Endured
6. Many P.C.'s
7. London lav
8. Vacuum's lack
9. Purifies
10. Not close
11. He taught an ancient language in film
12. Old London Magazine essayist
13. Celebrated Prohibition-era lawman
18. Tool with a cross handle
22. Feedbag feed
23. "Golden" things
24. Vanquished
25. What 17- and 52-Across and 11-Down all were
26. Curtain
27. North Carolina's ___ Banks
31. Some china
32. Church V.I.P.'s
34. Myopic cartoon character
37. Certain Boeing
38. Church music maker
40. Muslim pilgrimage
41. Arm bones
44. Spam producer
46. Adds punch to, as punch
48. Bygone auto
49. Toward shelter
50. Not pro
53. Commercial suffix with Motor
54. Biblical ark passenger
55. Ref's decision
56. 3-in-One product
57. "The Matrix" role

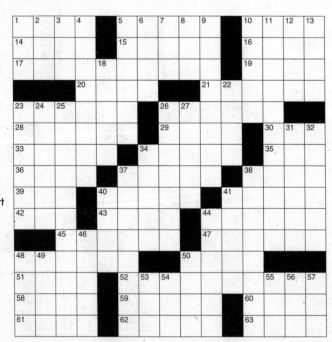

by Gene Newman

ACROSS
1 Drug buster
5 Eight furlongs
9 Fishermen's pailfuls
14 1998 Sarah McLachlan hit
15 Double agent Aldrich
16 Sleep disorder
17 Fake cover stories
19 "Bad" for "good," e.g.
20 Dress with a flare
21 Stephen Foster classic
23 Back of the boat
25 Key of Beethoven's Symphony No. 7: Abbr.
27 Attacked with zeal
28 Not nerdy
30 Bikini blast, briefly
32 Stumblers' sounds
33 Get a program on the radio
35 Mars explorer
37 Homeric epic
38 Familiar Olympics chant
39 King protectors
43 Watch
45 Catch between bases, say
46 K.C.-to-Little Rock direction
48 Surveyors' calculations
50 ___ Stanley Gardner
51 Grand
53 Equine quipster
55 Airline to Amsterdam
56 Hermit
58 Omnium-gatherums
60 Running wild
61 Shocked response in conversation
65 Reaches over
66 Move, in Realtor-speak
67 Easy gait
68 "Roots" writer
69 Once, once upon a time
70 Hightailed it

DOWN
1 Get the drop on
2 Stir
3 Tubes on the table
4 Being the reason for
5 Best bro
6 Pooped person's plaint
7 Pacific ring
8 "Happy Motoring" company
9 Méphistophélès player in "Faust"
10 Valedictorian's feat, perhaps
11 Comparatively cockamamie
12 Court contest
13 "Contact" astronomer
18 ___ Fail (Irish coronation stone)
22 Modern viewer's option, briefly
23 When Hamlet sees his father's ghost
24 Cager's offense
26 Destination for many pilgrims
29 "Three's a crowd"
31 March master
34 Exiled Amin
36 Org. concerned with PCB's
38 Onetime TWA rival
40 Place with sawdust
41 Zero
42 Leaf holder
44 Gallivants
45 J. Alfred Prufrock poet
46 Himalayan guide
47 Mixer
49 Wakeup calls
51 Riffraff
52 Cracked
54 Performed
57 Fictional Jane
59 Barn birds
62 Donne's "done"
63 Big brute
64 Koppel of ABC

by Nancy Salomon and Levi Denham

ACROSS

1 Tree that people carve their initials in
6 Pepper's partner
10 Author Dinesen
14 Stevenson of 1950's politics
15 Dunkable cookie
16 Plot parcel
17 "Dee-licious!"
19 Alum
20 Carson's predecessor on "The Tonight Show"
21 Surgeon's outfit
23 Play parts
26 Goes to sleep, with "off"
29 Skirt lines
30 Bangkok native
31 Like snow after a blizzard, perhaps
33 Corrosions
35 Eyelid problem
36 Spanish aunt
39 Crying
42 Evangeline or Anna Karenina, e.g.
44 What candles sometimes represent
45 "Very funny!"
47 Animal nose
48 Show biz parent
52 Go left or right
53 Petri dish filler
54 Where the Himalayas are
55 Not in port
56 Main arteries
58 Den
60 High spirits
61 "Dee-licious!"
67 Fanny
68 Certain woodwind
69 Pitcher Martinez
70 Painting and sculpting, e.g.
71 Yards advanced
72 Animal in a roundup

DOWN

1 San Francisco/ Oakland separator
2 School's Web site address ender
3 Shade tree
4 Where a tent is pitched
5 "Howdy!"
6 Grow sick of
7 Quarterback's asset
8 Moon lander, for short
9 Santa's sackful
10 "Amen!"
11 "Dee-licious!"
12 Saudis and Iraqis
13 Classic sneakers
18 American, abroad
22 Bar "where everybody knows your name"
23 Skylit lobbies
24 Newswoman Connie
26 "Dee-licious!"
27 ___ Moines
28 Genesis son
32 Color, as an Easter egg
34 African desert
37 Get used (to)
38 MetLife competitor
40 Scandal sheet
41 Where the Mets can be met
43 Perfectly precise
46 Mornings, briefly
49 Spuds
50 Some Texas tycoons
51 "Just the facts, ___"
53 One who hears "You've got mail"
56 Taj Mahal site
57 Urban haze
59 Little devils
62 Entrepreneur's deg.
63 "Who, me?"
64 "___ to Joy"
65 Mine find
66 "Le Coq ___"

by Nancy Salomon and Kyle Mahowald

ACROSS

1 Sharp-eyed raptor
6 Kid's getaway
10 Military level
14 Lamebrain
15 Off base illegally
16 "Garfield" dog
17 "The Godfather" actor's reputation?
19 Umpteen
20 UFO fliers
21 Novelist Zane
22 River under London Bridge, once
24 Alfalfa, Spanky and others
26 Tibia's place
27 Christian pop singer Grant
28 Camera-friendly events
32 Cheap jewelry
35 Rapunzel's abundance
36 Off-key, in a way
37 Garage occupant
38 "It ain't over till it's over" speaker
39 Gawk at
40 Beach sidler
41 New York City's ___ River
42 Comprehend
43 Arrange in columns
45 Old French coin
46 Rolling in the dough
47 Stops talking suddenly
51 Pants measure
54 Soccer success
55 Expert
56 Fan club's honoree
57 U2 singer's journey?
60 Indian tourist site
61 River to the Caspian
62 Lecture jottings
63 Posterior
64 Kittens' cries
65 Dress to kill, with "up"

DOWN

1 Fireplace glower
2 Line from the heart
3 Wimbledon court surface
4 Actor Chaney
5 Final stage, in chess
6 Yuletide sweets
7 On vacation
8 S.U.V. "chauffeur," maybe
9 Overabundance
10 Actor Ray's discussion group?
11 First mate?
12 "The Whole ___ Yards"
13 Florida islets
18 Air France destination
23 Chart topper
25 Roman statesman's thieving foe?
26 Tank top, e.g.
28 Analyze, as a sentence
29 Gymnast Korbut
30 Buddies
31 Put one's foot down?
32 Hostilities ender
33 Subtle glow
34 Attempt
35 Shrubby tract
38 Lauderdale loafer
42 Cooperate (with)
44 Soused
45 Pole or Bulgarian
47 Puts on ice
48 Petty quarrels
49 More than suggests
50 Metrical verse
51 Tall tale teller
52 Upper hand
53 Writer Ephron
54 Chew like a rat
58 Vein contents
59 "___ rang?"

by Lynn Lempel

Note: Each of the three theme answers below (20-, 36- and 54-Across) can be clued with the same three letters.

ACROSS

1 Chick on the piano
6 P.D.Q. in the I.C.U.
10 Casing
14 Ph.D. hurdle
15 Part of "S.N.L."
16 Narrow way
17 Try to bite
18 Mental flash
19 Aboard
20 [See instructions]
23 Flamenco shout
24 Sushi selection
25 Comb stopper
27 Harangues
30 Toward the tail
32 Copacabana site
33 Youth
34 Dedicated lines?
35 Kennel sound
36 [See instructions]
41 Leave the scene
42 Satisfy the munchies
43 50-50, e.g.
44 Old discs
45 Orthodontist, for one: Abbr.
46 Calls the shots
50 Words of assistance
52 Sidekick
53 Cry of insight
54 [See instructions]
59 Cork's country
60 Confess
61 Camel caravan's stop-off
62 Tend the sauce
63 Victory goddess
64 Advil alternative
65 Caribbean and others
66 Rock radio pioneer Freed
67 Administered medicine

DOWN

1 Swindle
2 Yankee opponent
3 Cousin of an épée
4 Zing
5 Vino region
6 Covers with gunk
7 Kind of basin
8 State firmly
9 Sign of sorrow
10 "Wake of the Ferry" painter
11 Pocket protector?
12 Cabinet post since 1849
13 Opposite of paleo-
21 Ribbed
22 Follower's suffix
26 Barn section
28 Heaps
29 Letter from Greece
30 Flap
31 Productive
34 Frequently, in verse
35 "Whoopee!"
36 Healthy
37 Speed up
38 Ornamental vine: Var.
39 "___ Kapital"
40 What a person may become when kneeling
45 Society newbie
46 Obscure
47 Political movements
48 Prosper
49 Got fresh with
51 Mike who played Austin Powers
52 Lawrence Welk specialty
55 Sicilian hothead?
56 Come up short
57 Loathsome person
58 Sign of sanctity
59 Double curve

by Richard Silvestri

ACROSS

1 Tow
5 From County Clare, e.g.
10 ___ pet (onetime fad item)
14 "The Thin Man" pooch
15 Off-limits
16 "Crazy" bird
17 Manual transmission
19 "What've you been ___?"
20 Politely
21 High-spirited horse
23 Swap
24 From one side to the other
26 Shade of beige
28 Warwick who sang "Walk On By"
32 Tree branch
36 Makes a row in a garden, say
38 "Hasta la vista!"
39 Operatic solo
40 Academy Award
42 Fighting, often with "again"
43 Goes off on a mad tangent
45 With 22-Down, Korea's location
46 Bone-dry
47 Moose or mouse
49 Perlman of "Cheers"
51 Upstate New York city famous for silverware
53 Twinkie's filling
58 Versatile legume
61 Entraps
62 Jai ___
63 Lakeshore rental, perhaps
66 Lass
67 Between, en français

68 Taking a break from work
69 One of two wives of Henry VIII
70 Hem again
71 Loch ___ monster

DOWN

1 Lacks, quickly
2 Up and about
3 Ancient city NW of Carthage
4 Tied, as shoes
5 ___-bitsy
6 Shout from the bleachers
7 There: Lat.
8 Until now
9 Souped-up car
10 Standard drink mixers
11 Arizona tribe
12 Tiny amount
13 Shortly

18 Swiss artist Paul ___
22 See 45-Across
24 Came up
25 What a TV host reads from
27 Funnywoman Margaret
29 Evening, in ads
30 Dark film genre, informally
31 Villa d'___
32 "___ Croft Tomb Raider" (2001 film)
33 Tehran's land
34 Prefix with skirt or series
35 Transportation for the Dynamic Duo
37 Bird's name in "Peter and the Wolf"
41 Numbered rd.

44 Of sound mind
48 Frog, at times
50 Unappealing skin condition
52 Idiotic
54 1990's Israeli P.M.
55 Wear away
56 Breakfast, lunch and dinner
57 Kefauver of 1950's politics
58 "Star Wars" for one
59 Actress Lena
60 Folksy tale
61 Whole bunch
64 Alcoholic's woe
65 Rapper Dr. ___

by Jeffrey Harris

ACROSS

1 New stable arrival
5 Wrigley team
9 Beginning
14 Old Dodge model
15 Pronto!
16 Captain Nemo's creator
17 Jared of "Panic Room"
18 "A ___ formality!"
19 Chip away at
20 Winter accessory
23 Up to, in ads
24 Coll., e.g.
25 However, informally
28 Caffeine source for many
33 Learn about
35 The whole shebang
36 Forest canine
38 Sailing hazards
41 Geo. W. Bush has one
42 Artfully dodge
43 Simple door fastener
46 Price word
47 Black-and-orange songbird
48 Polite drivers, at merges
51 Columbia Univ. locale
52 Something to shuck
54 ___ de Cologne
55 What the ends of 20-, 36- and 43-Across suggest
61 Language of India
64 Actress Malone
65 Tea time, perhaps
66 French farewell
67 Wide-eyed
68 Book after II Chronicles
69 1692 witch trials city
70 Fine-tune
71 For fear that

DOWN

1 Arlo Guthrie's genre
2 Spilled salt, say
3 Pro's foe
4 Ray of "GoodFellas"
5 The Kennedy years, figuratively
6 Played for a sap
7 3 Musketeers units
8 Eyeglasses, informally
9 "Yoo-hoo!"
10 Soft ball material
11 Sellout indicator
12 Cut short
13 Pigskin prop
21 Part of three-in-a-row
22 Yearn (for)
25 Minstrel show group
26 Player in extra-point attempts
27 Job seekers' good news
28 Graphite element
29 Legendary Mrs. who owned a cow
30 Frock wearer
31 Arm or leg
32 Perth ___, N.J.
34 Piercing tool
37 Java neighbor
39 To's partner
40 Element #34
44 First wife of Jacob
45 Like many MTV viewers
49 Slip behind
50 Camper's bag
53 Indian prince
55 ___ fixe (obsession)
56 Toy block maker
57 Get ___ the ground floor
58 Gooey stuff
59 Sharer's word
60 "Dang!"
61 Is afflicted with
62 Actress Lupino
63 Zip

by Nancy Kavanaugh

ACROSS

1 Holiday visitor, maybe
6 Sporty car, for short
10 Plum NASCAR position
14 Western necktie?
15 Crashing sort
16 Hera's mother
17 Knew
20 Dish cooked in a pot
21 Trim, in a way
22 Key material
23 Ludwig Mies van der ___
25 Gospel writer
27 New
33 Prefix with arthritis
34 Forum greeting
35 Brought up
37 Mao's successor
38 Alistair who wrote "Ice Station Zebra"
42 Put away
43 Ex-D.C. baseballers
45 See 27-Down
46 Derby place
48 Nu
52 Rough tool
53 Kitchen flooring, for short
54 Scarecrow's composition
57 Viking's deity
59 Bubble wrap sounds
63 Gnu
66 Feels punk
67 Peace Nobelist Ducommun
68 2000 N.B.A. M.V.P.
69 Spymaster's worry
70 Rx amts.
71 Famous "hostess with the mostest"

DOWN

1 Poop
2 Seasonal air
3 Veg out
4 Fertility goddess
5 Chinese dynasty name
6 Homes
7 Like a Hail Mary pass
8 Woodstock phenomenon
9 1950's political initials
10 Poor Richard's Almanack item
11 "You gotta be kidding!"
12 Wolf's look
13 "Duck soup!"
18 Classic soft drink
19 Triathlete's need
24 Baseball's Blue Moon
26 Iris's place
27 With 45-Across, noted Arctic explorer
28 Bar order, with "the"
29 ___ Department
30 Novelist Carr
31 Wipe out
32 Dry out, informally
36 Prefix with god
39 Bellicose god
40 HOV lane users
41 It's inert
44 Berlin boulevard
47 Barbecuer's buy
49 Fancy marbles
50 Skips over
51 50's car features
54 Ponzi scheme, e.g.
55 Cream was one
56 Frank holder
58 Socially challenged sort
60 Reveals, in verse
61 Survey map
62 Ward of the screen
64 Rainy
65 Author Clancy

by Jim Conklin

ACROSS

1 Child by marriage
8 Downtown Chicago
15 Percentage listed in an I.R.S. booklet
16 "Good shot!"
17 Woman who's "carrying"
19 Anger, with "up"
20 Summer: Fr.
21 Coin opening
22 Lottery player's exultant cry
23 Obstreperous
26 Wash
27 Put on board, as cargo
28 ___ constrictor
29 Bits of land in la Méditerranée
30 Ogled
31 Yankee Stadium locale, with "the"
33 Role
34 "Vive ___!" (old French cheer)
35 Trail
39 Uncles'. mates
40 Shakespearean king
44 On the ocean
45 Schubert's Symphony No. 8 ___ Minor
46 Wheel turner
47 Pie pans
48 Patronizes a library
51 Italian resort on the Adriatic
52 Founded: Abbr.
53 Bill Clinton's relig. affiliation
54 New-___ (devotee of crystals and incense)
55 Traditional end of summer

60 Lenders, often
61 International alliance
62 Summed
63 Appetizer

DOWN

1 Germless
2 What a plane rolls along
3 Go off, as a bomb
4 Dressed up in a fussy way
5 Anatomical pouch
6 Playful aquatic animal
7 "Pretty amazing!"
8 Boom producer, for short
9 "She Done ___ Wrong"

10 Environmental prefix
11 Accidentally reveal
12 "Sexy!"
13 Bogey, in golf
14 Most cheeky
18 Maternity ward arrival
24 Start of a forbiddance
25 Vertical line on a graph
31 British P.M. Tony
32 Get together with old classmates, say
35 Kneecap
36 "Let me repeat . . ."
37 Covered place to sleep
38 Committed, as an act

40 Staples Center player, for short
41 Requiring immediate attention
42 Somewhat firm, as pasta
43 Organize differently, as troops
49 1920's vice president Charles
50 Paid out
56 Wand
57 R & B band ___ Hill
58 Nile viper
59 Greek letter

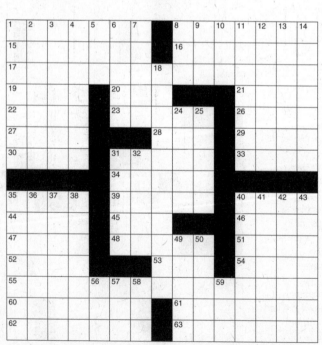

by Michael Shteyman

ACROSS

1 Kind of boom
6 Celeste who won an Oscar for "Gentleman's Agreement"
10 Ticks off
14 "Love Story" author Segal
15 Tribe defeated by the Iroquois
16 Webster who had a way with words
17 Point between Hawaii and Guam
19 Center of a cathedral
20 Mine find
21 Chem. or biol.
22 Narrowed
24 Snapple rival
26 Mary ___ Moore
27 "Oklahoma!" aunt
29 Eye holder
33 Knock out of the sky
36 Pick a card
38 Actress Foch and others
39 "Pumping ___"
40 Divans
42 Civil rights activist Parks
43 Money substitute
45 The end ___ era
46 "Good buddy"
47 Dorothy's home in "The Wizard of Oz"
49 Poker player's declaration
51 Doubting Thomas
53 Spanish dish
57 Silt, e.g.
60 Stick in the water?
61 Crest alternative
62 Jacob's twin
63 Hock shop receipt
66 Ado
67 Gen. Robt. ___
68 "There ___ free lunches"
69 Reporter Clark
70 Some loaves
71 Limb holder?

DOWN

1 Attach, as a patch
2 "___ Ben Jonson" (literary epitaph)
3 Alternatives to Reeboks
4 Rocks at the bar
5 Sculpt
6 Prefix with port or pad
7 ___ pro nobis
8 Like a dryer trap
9 Some awards
10 Group of confidants
11 Surf's sound
12 Gutter location
13 Place for a mower
18 Heats just short of boiling
23 Unskilled laborer
25 Place for sets and lets
26 Word that can precede the last word of 17- and 63-Across and 10- and 25-Down
28 Suffix with switch
30 Door opener
31 Facilitate
32 Russian leader before 1917
33 Tiddlywink, e.g.
34 Shamu, for one
35 Slightly tattered
37 Female W.W. II grp.
41 Attack verbally
44 Settles up
48 Concealed shooter
50 Rodeo rope
52 "Boot" in the Mediterranean
54 Los Angeles player
55 Property claims
56 Response to "Are not!"
57 Office necessity
58 Villa d'___
59 What an analgesic stops
60 Addition column
64 Minute
65 ___-Magnon

by Sarah Keller

ACROSS

1 Son of Judah
5 "Ba-da-___!"
9 Clearly
14 Baseball's Hideo ___
15 Words with a nod
16 Like Cro-Magnon man, to us
17 Got down
18 Keaton's "Mr. Mom" co-star
19 Struck from the Bible?
20 Narcissist's breakup line?
23 Fix, as old shoes
24 San Francisco's ___ Hill
25 Radio host's breakup line?
32 Audiophile's shelfful
35 One way to go to a party
36 "I understand, sir!"
37 Cupid's counterpart
39 Tease
41 First name in mystery
42 Easy to prepare, say
45 Accurse
48 Get-up-and-go
49 Astronaut's breakup line?
52 1988 Meg Ryan film
53 Cotton Bowl city
57 Farmer's breakup line?
62 Breakfast sizzler
63 Korea's Syngman ___
64 Retin-A treats it
65 Rod-shaped germ
66 Till slot
67 John Astin's actor son
68 They're verboten
69 Thai restaurant cookware
70 Rice-shaped pasta

DOWN

1 Sign in a station
2 Nick of "The Deep"
3 Out of place
4 "Later!"
5 Center of a circus
6 "Because ___ so!"
7 Fictional Wolfe
8 "-ing" word
9 Gaffer's aide
10 Traditional Thanksgiving dish
11 Word on a gift tag
12 Old, to Oskar
13 White alternative
21 Arena yells
22 Smidgen
26 Pencil holder
27 "Zounds!"
28 Ball holder
29 Org. for boomers, now
30 Singer Lovett
31 Stay fresh
32 Filmmaker Riefenstahl
33 Figurehead's place
34 Crash site?
38 Light source
40 Old Navy's parent, with "The"
43 France's patron
44 It might make you short of breath
46 March ___ (47-Down tourney)
47 School sports org.
50 Peter of Peter, Paul and Mary
51 Rio Grande city
54 Football factory worker
55 Ball's partner
56 Pool member of old
57 Baylor's city
58 B-school subj.
59 Electrical unit
60 "This can't be!"
61 Pay period
62 Rose's home

by Steve Jones

ACROSS

1 Raindrop sound
5 Sgt., e.g.
8 Present for a teacher
13 Kelly of morning TV
14 Marlboro alternative
15 Shine
16 Son of Isaac
17 Metal that Superman can't see through
18 On again, as a candle
19 Fashionable London locale
21 Ardor
22 Big containers
23 Filmmaker Spike
24 GM sports car
27 Whitewater part of a stream
30 Fireplace accessory
32 UK record label
33 Cast member
36 Hits head-on
37 Get help of a sort on "Who Wants to Be a Millionaire"
41 Wriggling fishes
42 Place
43 Tit for ___
44 Teems
47 Zoo denizens
49 Something "on the books"
50 Motorists' grp.
51 Skier's transport
52 Quick job for a barber
54 Sweater
58 To no ___ (purposelessly)
60 Classic artist's subject
61 Sandwich spread, for short
62 Oscar who wrote "The Picture of Dorian Gray"
63 Popular shirt label
64 Certain stock index
65 Los Angeles cager
66 Craggy hill
67 Agile

DOWN

1 Make ready, for short
2 Elvis's daughter ___ Marie
3 Milky gem
4 1960's–70's pontiff
5 December songs
6 Fuel from a mine
7 Bygone
8 Consented
9 Bit of begging
10 Educational assistance since 1972
11 China's Chou En-___
12 Expert in resuscitation, in brief
14 Coffee gathering
20 Angry with
21 ___ state (blissful self-awareness)
23 Lash of old westerns
25 Frisky feline
26 Beginnings
27 Statute removal
28 Itsy-bitsy creature
29 Bedtime gab
31 Anger
34 Actress Allen of "Enough"
35 Cheerios grain
38 Baton Rouge sch.
39 Tried a little of this, a little of that
40 Rarely-met goal
45 Hammer user
46 Hoover ___
48 Scents
51 Henry VIII's family name
53 Travel on horseback
54 Mario who wrote "The Godfather"
55 Seductress
56 Witness
57 Classic theater name
58 Leatherworker's tool
59 By way of
60 Annual hoops contest, for short

by Jay Giess

ACROSS

1 Dispensable candy
4 On pins and needles
8 Meeting
14 "The Name of the Rose" writer
15 Chaucer offering
16 1966 Mary Martin musical
17 Dog with an upturned tail
19 Big-time brat
20 Sluggin' Sammy
21 Glasgow gal
23 Master's worker
24 Gambler's marker
26 Choice word
29 Give one's word
35 Beantown team, briefly
36 Press release?
37 Santa ___, Calif.
38 Holder of two tablets
39 Mingling with
42 Camera type, briefly
43 Taoism founder Lao-___
44 Horror film staple
45 Site of a racing win or a tie
47 Traditional elocution exercise
51 Beheaded Boleyn
52 Den denizen
53 Injure seriously
56 Limp watch painter
58 Sci-fi sightings
62 Take stock of
65 Intellectual
67 Fire escape, e.g.
68 Turkish honorific
69 Clean air grp.
70 Be obsequious
71 One of the "Little Women"
72 Letters for a psychic

DOWN

1 They're above the abs
2 It might be off the wall
3 Animal keepers
4 And so on: Abbr.
5 Veronica Lake film "The Blue ___"
6 What a poor winner does
7 They have boughs for bows
8 Peach part
9 Words from Wordsworth
10 Go downhill
11 Put a traveling mike on
12 Reason for nose-pinching
13 Klingon on the Enterprise
18 Odd fellow
22 Baseball commissioner Bud
25 Honeycomb shape
27 Periscope part
28 "The Bartered Bride" composer
29 Trunk with a chest
30 Out of kilter
31 Dog tag datum
32 Explorer ___ da Gama
33 Not at full power
34 Job for a dermatologist
35 Ordeal for Rover, perhaps
40 Like a trim lawn
41 Globular
46 Second-stringer
48 "Anything you want"
49 Make beholden
50 Scale reading
53 Halloween accessory
54 Concerning
55 Middle of Caesar's boast
57 "Moby-Dick" captain
59 Unbind
60 "My bad!"
61 Give and take
63 Sign of a sellout
64 Opposite NNE
66 "I told you so!"

by Nancy Salomon and Harvey Estes

ACROSS

1 Potato chip, to a Brit
6 Willy Wonka's creator
10 Little ones
14 Year-end temp
15 Plane measure
16 City south of Moscow
17 A pronoun has one
19 Bit of cunning
20 "The Omega Man" star, 1971
21 New arrival, of sorts
23 Maureen Dowd piece
25 "Get a grip!"
27 Straw source
28 60's trip cause
29 Teutonic surname starter
30 Chest item
31 Astronomical discovery of 1930
33 Somber song
35 "Ruthless People" star
39 Tony winner Swoosie
40 African antelope
43 Rover's warning
46 Former U.S. mil. acronym
47 Big poker player's wager
49 Clinch
50 Engage in woolgathering?
53 Old TV problem
54 Military surprise
55 No longer in effect
57 Box lightly
58 Battle cry
62 Narcissist's love
63 Came down

64 Knock senseless
65 Poker player's calculation
66 Famous rhymer of Bronx with "thonx"
67 Aggressive sort

DOWN

1 Lee's org.
2 Sought a seat
3 Taking a bath
4 Tilter's mount
5 Donation-soliciting grps.
6 Set into a groove
7 Where the action is
8 Farm layer
9 Up-to-the-minute news
10 Namely
11 Properly

12 Texas border city
13 Hazardous for driving, maybe
18 J.F.K. postings
22 Was sociable, in a way
23 Alley ___
24 Bud
26 Mid first-century year
28 "Odyssey" morsels
32 Shatner sci-fi drug
33 Noncombat area, for short
34 Electric ___
36 "Circular file"
37 Use acid
38 Start of a deluge
41 One above a specialist: Abbr.
42 It may become hoarfrost

43 Former Connecticut governor Ella
44 Wheelchair-accessible
45 Like Playboy cartoons
47 The haves have it
48 Date with an M.D.
51 Browses, today
52 Perry of fashion
53 Serta rival
56 Wishy-washy
59 Taking after
60 Cohort of Curly
61 Sp. lady

by Alan Arbesfeld

ACROSS

1 Go to sea
5 Feet above sea level: Abbr.
9 Boston's airport
14 Stubborn animal
15 Ear part
16 Ex-Mrs. Trump
17 Fitzgerald who sang "I'm Making Believe"
18 University V.I.P.
19 Car parker
20 Decreed
23 ___ foil
24 Before, in verse
25 Fleming of 007 fame
26 Bad mark
28 Discontinued
29 Lacking muscle
33 Writer Welty
35 Throng
36 Document of legal representation
40 Liqueur flavoring
41 Armadas
42 Nary a soul
43 Injection units, for short
44 Relaxed
48 Tree swinger
49 Joanne of "Sylvia," 1965
50 1959 hit song about "a man named Charlie"
51 Children's game
56 Easy gallops
57 Bad place to drop a heavy box
58 Landed (on)
59 Florida city
60 Advantage
61 Ready for picking
62 Like sea air
63 Flagmaker Betsy
64 1930's boxer Max

DOWN

1 Refines, as metal
2 How some café is served
3 "Fighting" Big Ten team
4 Starring role
5 Fabled New World city
6 "Camelot" composer
7 Israel's Abba
8 Open the windows in
9 Jazz up
10 Running track
11 Festive party
12 Again
13 ___ King Cole
21 Shy
22 "This ___ better be good!"
27 Honkers
28 Rigorous exams
29 On the downslide
30 Sea eagle
31 Lemon or lime drink
32 C minor, for one
34 Unbalanced
35 Spa feature
36 Criticize, as a movie
37 Plastic ___ Band
38 Victory
39 Fragrant flowers
43 Overseer of co. books
45 Earhart who disappeared over the Pacific
46 Skunk feature
47 It immediately follows Passiontide
48 Examine, as ore
49 Bottom of the barrel
51 ___-Cola
52 Iridescent stone
53 Skin
54 One slow on the uptake
55 Cutting remark
56 The "L" of L.A.

by A. J. Santora

ACROSS

1 Unconsciousness
5 Govt. security
10 Tell all
14 Eve's mate
15 North of talk radio
16 Leave in the dust
17 Player of Ginger
19 A few chips in the pot, maybe
20 Kind of scene in a movie
21 Other, to Ortega
22 Inspirations
23 Player of the title role in 37-Across
26 [Woe is me!]
30 Social historian Jacob
31 Charles Lamb, pseudonymously
32 Desist
34 Ewe's cry
37 Classic sitcom that debuted on 9/26/1964
41 ___ sauce
42 Blue-haired lady of TV cartoons
43 Ye ___ Shoppe
44 7-Eleven, e.g.
45 Adorable "bears"
47 Player of Thurston Howell III
50 Half-man/half-goat creatures
52 ___-majesté
53 Org. that helps with motel discounts
56 Remark while putting chips in the pot
57 Player of the Skipper
60 Mexican fast food
61 Mob
62 "I smell ___!"
63 Slow-boil

64 Got up
65 Hunky-___

DOWN

1 See 3-Down
2 "Garfield" dog
3 With 1-Down, tailless pets
4 Doctor's org.
5 Overly
6 Squib on a book jacket
7 Ancient Greek class reading
8 Fleur-de-___
9 Name that's a homophone of 8-Down
10 Shivs
11 Society avoider
12 Nick and Nora's pooch
13 Spelling contests
18 Gray wolf

22 Harvard, Yale, Princeton, etc., for short
24 Rub out
25 Not yet final, at law
26 Importunes
27 Mixture
28 Greasy
29 Actor Linden or Holbrook
32 Magna ___
33 Essay writer's class: Abbr.
34 Shiny on top?
35 "Three Men ___ Baby"
36 Summer drinks
38 Some prayer leaders
39 Dress
40 Actor Chaney
44 Boat on 37-Across

45 Shoved
46 Lost
47 Result of squeezing, maybe
48 Mild cigar
49 Japanese form of fencing
50 Partner of starts
51 Latin 101 verb
53 Prefix with nautical
54 Slightly open
55 Creative
57 Responses to a masseur
58 Home stretch?
59 Irish fellow

by Andrea Carla Michaels

ACROSS

1 Code word for "A"
5 Jostle
10 Mockery
14 Blackens
15 Model Gabrielle
16 "Unimaginable as ___ in Heav'n": Milton
17 Understood
18 Popular 80's–90's TV sitcom
20 "Let's Make ___"
22 Elton John, e.g.
23 Clarinetist Shaw
24 ___ the world
26 A different approach
28 Slalom course move
29 William who has a state named after him
31 Slippery sort
32 Lulu
34 Shakes up
36 In case that's true
40 Olin of "Hollywood Homicide," 2003
41 Charge
42 "___ and Lovers" (D. H. Lawrence book)
43 Italian wine-growing region
44 1973 #1 Rolling Stones hit
45 Chisel or gouge
46 Big maker of A.T.M.'s
48 Yes ___
50 Cube root of eight
51 Monkey business
55 Blown snow
57 Midwest home of ConAgra
58 Corp. money head
60 Holy ___

62 Tumbler
65 Halo
66 Newsman Sevareid
67 Sauce with jalapeño
68 Any of the Phillies, e.g.
69 Winter Olympics venue
70 Oversized volume
71 "___ Heartache" (Bonnie Tyler hit)

DOWN

1 Aleutian island
2 Hidden dangers
3 Player without a contract
4 Dam on the Nile
5 Suffix with east
6 Island rings
7 September equinox, and a hint to the starts of 18- & 62-Across and 2-, 3-, 10-, 33-, 37- & 38-Down
8 Yellow shade
9 Dewy
10 Place for a select group
11 High-class, as a restaurant
12 Take ___ (travel)
13 Allots, with "out"
19 Lawyer's undertaking
21 Cut (off)
25 Maserati competitor
27 London theater district
28 "La Débâcle" novelist
30 Verb preceder
33 Consolation of a sort

35 Den
37 Court infraction
38 Winter driving aid
39 See 64-Down
47 Blacken
49 Assn.
51 Lawn Boy product
52 Japanese porcelain
53 Audited, with "on"
54 Conspicuous success
56 Shiraz native
59 Greek peak
61 Boris Pasternak heroine
63 Fed. construction overseer
64 Airline to 39-Down

by David J. Kahn

ACROSS

1 Leaf's support
5 Knife
9 Wood for chests
14 Like a lemon
15 Medal of honor recipient
16 "Stayin'___" (disco hit)
17 Prison sentence
18 Therefore
19 Without a stitch on
20 Eventually
23 The "M" in MSG
24 Calif.'s northern neighbor
25 Ewe's mate
28 Main school team
31 Valedictorian's pride, for short
34 Make amends (for)
36 Ubiquitous bug
37 QB Tarkenton
38 Daring bet
42 Whom Ingrid played in "Casablanca"
43 Pea container
44 Many a John Wayne film
45 Spanish cheer
46 Most sore
49 Tricky
50 Title car in a 1964 pop hit
51 Have to have
53 Availability extremes
59 Alaskan islander
60 Lifeguard's watch
61 "___ honest with you . . ."
63 The vowel sound in "dude"
64 That girl, in Paris
65 Problem with a fishing line
66 Excited, with "up"
67 Funnyman Foxx
68 Stringed toy

DOWN

1 Jet decommissioned in '03
2 They may get stepped on
3 Continental "dollar"
4 1983 role reversal film
5 The Ramones' "___ Is a Punk Rocker"
6 Extreme fear
7 Jason's ship, in myth
8 Unmannered fellow
9 Bird in a cage
10 Gladden
11 Dutch embankment
12 Swear to
13 Bloodshot
21 "The Catcher in the Rye," e.g.
22 Game with a drawing
25 The "R" of N.P.R.
26 Polynesian island
27 Cat's quarry
29 Noted New York restaurateur
30 A home away from home
31 Southern breakfast dish
32 Discussion group
33 Incensed
35 Hoops grp.
37 Home loan agcy.
39 Disney's ___ Center
40 "That feels good!"
41 Carving on a pole
46 Offered for breeding, as a thoroughbred
47 Wrap up
48 Made airtight
50 Measuring tool
52 Scatterbrained
53 Ice sheet
54 Start of a counting-out rhyme
55 0 on a phone: Abbr.
56 Play part
57 Talking on a cell phone during a movie, e.g.
58 On-line auction house
59 Chemical base: Abbr.
62 Swellheadedness

by Gregory Paul

ACROSS

1 ___-serve
5 Desert flora
10 Fresh kid
14 Jacob's twin
15 Venusian, e.g.
16 Suffix with Cine-
17 T ___ tiger
18 Muscle injuries
19 Lyric poems
20 Protest formally
23 Not well
24 Silver ___ (cloud seed)
25 Before now
28 Cry out loud
30 Moon or sun, poetically
31 Diet plate serving
36 Falco of "The Sopranos"
37 Battery type
38 Siberian city
41 Cockpit gauge figure
46 ___ Ronald Reagan
47 In the style of
48 Go astray
49 Moral standards
53 A smartypants may have a big one
55 Cohabitate
62 Juan's emphatic assent
63 Actress Verdugo
64 Ocean motion
65 Penny-___ (trivial)
66 Aired again
67 Caesarean rebuke
68 Time to go once around the sun
69 Peter, Paul or Mary
70 Invitation letters

DOWN

1 One seen playing with a beachball
2 Logo along U.S. highways, once
3 Placed
4 Mold and mildew, for two
5 Former Sears mailing
6 A Baldwin
7 "See ya!"
8 Semester, e.g.
9 Fill with confidence
10 Like a sombrero's brim
11 Pie chart lines
12 Make better
13 "Take a sip"
21 Lanchester of film
22 Stud site
25 Air force hero
26 1977 George Burns title role
27 Ear-related
29 Trivial amount, slangily
30 Tara name
32 Mad Hatter's drink
33 Salary max
34 Message from a desert isle, perhaps
35 Cousins of an ostrich
39 ___ Lanka
40 Barbie's ex-beau
42 Simoleon
43 Publishers
44 Swanky
45 Herb in stuffing
49 Op-ed piece, e.g.
50 Quaker's "yours"
51 "___ la vista!"
52 Not so cordial
54 Riverbank romper
56 Courtroom statement
57 Actress Hatcher
58 ___ even keel
59 Half of a batting average calculation
60 1999 Ron Howard comedy
61 Do another hitch

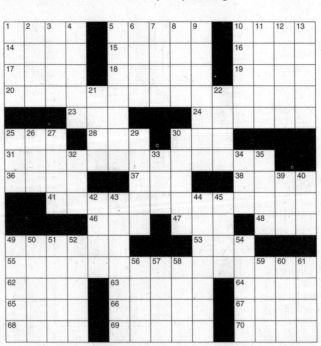

by Nancy Kavanaugh

ACROSS

1 Like most world table tennis champions
6 One who's been down the aisle
10 Sales caveat
14 "Ars ___ . . ."
15 Roman way
16 "Out with it!"
17 Ways up the slopes
18 Court plea, for short
19 Cameo stone
20 What friends said about 29-Across?
23 Bonanza find
24 Capp and Capone
25 Book before Esth.
26 Long-eared animal
29 Subject of this puzzle
32 Play's start
35 Like very narrow shoes
36 Opportunities, so to speak
37 Rubberneck
38 Nasty
41 Duff
42 "Peer Gynt" composer
44 L'homme over there
45 180's
46 What 29-Across might say about a good joke
50 Like very wide shoes
51 Item worn around the neck
52 A.T.M. need
53 Give a nickname
56 29-Across's political aspiration?
60 Mine, in Marseille
62 Cross letters
63 ___ sprawl

64 Artworks
65 Dodge compact
66 Actress Witherspoon
67 Pubmates
68 Sailor's drink
69 Cousins of harps

DOWN

1 Even if, succinctly
2 Off the sauce
3 Blown away
4 Indian tourist city
5 Capital of the Bahamas
6 Plane stat
7 Words of agreement
8 Grand theft auto, e.g.
9 Chipped away at
10 Wide-eyed
11 City on a strait
12 Wrigley Field flora
13 "___ sells" (advertising catchphrase)
21 Soprano Gluck and others
22 Israel's Barak
27 Leave the flock
28 Methods: Abbr.
29 Outdoorsman of a sort
30 Pre-kickoff call
31 Tend to a spill
32 Cow college student
33 Bill of fare
34 Like Hawthorne's "Tales"
39 Won ton, e.g.
40 Kid's song refrain
43 Kotter of 70's TV

47 Dove's activity
48 Julie ___, the voice of Marge Simpson
49 Roll out
53 Rome's river
54 Have ___ of the jitters
55 Inheritance carriers
57 Villain's reception
58 Suffix with buck
59 Glenn of the Eagles
60 EarthLink alternative
61 War stat

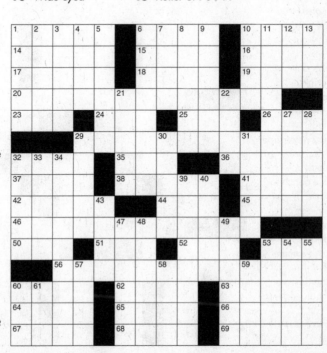

by Verna Suit

ACROSS

1 Used a broom
6 Opened just a crack
10 Doesn't guzzle
14 Place for a barbecue
15 "Uh-uh"
16 Threaded fastener
17 Proverb
18 Managed, with "out"
19 ___ avis (unusual one)
20 Bathroom fixture sales representative?
23 Way to the top of a mountain
26 Stave off
27 Hanging sculpture in Alabama?
32 Alleviated
33 Words said on the way out the door
34 E.M.T.'s skill
37 Pub drinks
38 Gasps for air
39 "Scram!"
40 Dashed
41 Sunday newspaper color feature
42 Continue downhill without pedaling
43 Warsaw refinement?
45 G-rated
48 Accustoms
49 Majestic summer time?
54 Solar emissions
55 Really big show
56 Lubricated
60 Victim of a prank
61 Choir voice
62 State fund-raiser

63 Retired fliers, for short
64 Spinks or Trotsky
65 Company in a 2001–02 scandal

DOWN

1 Hot springs locale
2 Bankroll
3 When a plane should get in: Abbr.
4 Dirty places
5 Initial progress on a tough problem
6 From a fresh angle
7 Wisecrack
8 Copycat
9 Cincinnati team
10 Endeavored
11 Dumbstruck
12 Less adulterated
13 Sudden jump
21 Be behind in payments
22 50/50 share
23 Besmirch
24 Down Under critter
25 "A Doll's House" playwright
28 Dolphins' venue
29 Onetime Dodges
30 Mess up
31 Contingencies
34 Committee head
35 Search party
36 Some I.R.A.'s, informally
38 One in the legislative biz
39 "Eureka!" cause
41 Swindles
42 TV cabinet
43 Purposes of commas
44 Little, in Lille
45 Deck of 52
46 Hawaiian feasts
47 "Aïda" setting
50 Bluish green
51 Car rod
52 "What've you been ___?"
53 Hired thug
57 Epistle: Abbr.
58 W.W. II arena
59 Underworld boss

by Seth A. Abel

ACROSS

1 Spills the beans
6 Got along
11 Epitome of simplicity
14 Accountants may run one
15 Entanglement
17 Said with a sneer
18 Garb for Tarzan
19 Eskimo building material
20 Bill of Rights defender, in brief
22 ___ voce (quietly)
23 "Maybellene" singer
27 Cries like a wolf
28 ___ Constitution
29 Three-legged piece
31 Stir up
34 Certain seat request
36 Suffix with fictional
39 Grimm brothers fairy tale
43 Popular fuel additive
44 Reveal
45 Openly mourned
46 Send (to)
48 Menu phrase
50 Lots and lots
52 Indirect
58 Inamoratas
60 Horn sound
61 Bearded animal
62 The starts of 18-, 23-, 39- and 52-Across
65 Spiral
67 Crystal-clear
68 Rugged ridge
69 Every other hurricane
70 Like music
71 Stallions' interests

DOWN

1 Underlying
2 Something for friends to "do"
3 A fond farewell
4 Wish
5 Butchers' offerings
6 Girl: Fr.
7 ___ propre
8 Baseball stat.
9 Sea eagle
10 Diagnosers
11 Similar
12 Itty-___
13 Some salmon
16 Boston newspaper
21 "CSI" network
24 Cosby's "I Spy" co-star
25 Amber or copal
26 Everyone, in the South
30 Toy train purchase
31 Trains: Abbr.
32 Passé
33 Not follow the book
34 Houston pro
35 "What was ___ think?"
37 Rush (along)
38 Tolkien creature
40 Jolly old ___ (Santa)
41 Lothario's look
42 Gun barrel cleaner
47 Other side
48 Big fuss
49 Philadelphia landmark hotel
50 French peaks
51 Religious parchment
53 Unadulterated
54 Pried (into)
55 Eyeballer
56 Conglomerate
57 Frequent Astaire wear
59 Genesis brother
63 Sebastian who once ran the world's fastest mile
64 Dos Passos work
66 Century 21 competitor

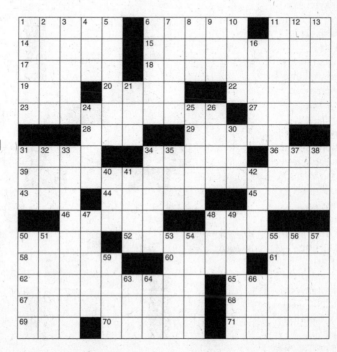

by James R. Leeds

ACROSS

1 Rockette launchers?
5 Combo's cue
10 Stereo knob
14 Like crazy
15 Cordial flavoring
16 With the bow, in music
17 "Kiss Me Kate" co-star, 1953
19 Time for a revolution
20 One of the Fab Four
21 State nicknamed "Small Wonder"
23 Mideast flash point
26 "The ___ Daba Honeymoon"
27 The Red Baron, e.g.
30 "Diner" actor
36 Press for payment
37 What well-thrown 44-Across do
38 This is one
39 Parasite supporter
41 Cambridge univ.
42 Seek food, per-haps
43 Sequel novel to "Typee"
44 Hail Marys, e.g.
47 Part of D.J.I.A.
48 1945 Peace Nobelist
50 Med. specialty
51 Certain invest-ment, for short
52 "La Vie en Rose" singer
54 Chinese potable
59 Driving hazard
63 Sit around
64 Utah senator
67 The Pointer Sisters' "___ Excited"
68 Pointed arch
69 Cut back
70 "Cold one"
71 Having bumps
72 Leave slack-jawed

DOWN

1 Lionized actor?
2 H. G. Wells race
3 Cap's partner
4 College football's Grand Old Man
5 Taken
6 Press, slangily
7 50-50, say
8 What a nod might mean
9 Spill one's guts
10 Show set in Hawaii
11 Atlas stat
12 Mark for life
13 Like some losers
18 Arteries
22 Six-pack ___
24 Sound on "Batman"
25 Brutish sort
27 Not permanent
28 Former New York governor
29 David of CNN
31 Dander
32 Really enjoys
33 Shake off
34 Yak, yak, yak . . .
35 Packaging abbr.
40 Super-delicious
44 1986 Best Picture
45 Quarterback Manning
46 More than trim
49 East ender?
53 Tries to fly
54 Like a slickster
55 Spanish Steps city
56 Facility
57 "Sum" preceder
58 Far from arable
60 Louis XIV, self-referentially
61 Linen hue
62 Not now
65 Stick-to-it-___
66 Sparks on the screen

by Adam Cohen

ACROSS

1 The "D" of D.J.
5 Huge hit
10 Nile reptiles
14 Great Salt Lake's state
15 Cosmetician Lauder
16 Junk e-mail
17 "The Price Is Right" phrase
19 Trig function
20 Eugene O'Neill's "___ for the Misbegotten"
21 Some necklines do this
23 Flatters, with "up"
26 Egypt's capital
27 2004 Olympics city
28 Made a cashless transaction
31 Accomplisher
32 Up, on a map
33 Chicago-to-Atlanta dir.
34 Factory-emissions testing grp.
35 "The Weakest Link" phrase
37 Photo ___ (picture-taking times)
38 Cotton ___
39 Bassoon's smaller cousins
40 Et ___ (and others)
41 Protective wear for airborne toxins
43 Wonder to behold
45 Nursery supplies
46 "___ Gump"
47 Oreo fillings
49 Wonderland cake message
50 Loooong sandwich
51 "Family Feud" phrase

56 Wading bird
57 Painting stand
58 Cafeteria carrier
59 Space shuttle launcher
60 Attire
61 "The ___ the limit"

DOWN

1 French nobleman
2 "How was ___ know?"
3 ___ Adams, patriot with a beer named after him
4 One peeking at answers on a test
5 Spanish gents
6 1980's PC's ran on it
7 Lots and lots
8 Finish, with "up"

9 All-female get-together
10 State confidently to
11 "Wheel of Fortune" phrase
12 Sign of hunger
13 "Peter Pan" pirate
18 Future indicator
22 Like a ballerina's body
23 No-goodnik
24 Paradise
25 "Jeopardy!" phrase
26 Atkins diet concerns, briefly
28 ___ well (is a good sign)
29 Glimpses
30 Make potable, as sea water
32 Partner of crannies
35 Flip out

36 Fanatical
40 Handcuffs
42 Brunch cocktail
43 Roadside stops
44 The Cadets, in college sports
46 Ones you just adore
47 Goatee's locale
48 Singer McEntire
49 Gaelic tongue
52 Former Mideast grp.
53 Noah's craft
54 Palindromic cheer
55 Part of CBS: Abbr.

by Jim Hyres

ACROSS

1 Asian nannies
6 Ending with land or sea
11 Legal org.
14 Josh ___, who directed and co-produced "South Pacific"
15 Inventor Howe
16 Right this minute
17 Skylit areas
18 Pipsqueaks
19 Genetic material
20 Items on some necklaces
22 Actor Estrada
23 Colorful tropical fish
24 Lacking vigor
26 Swing on an axis
29 Minor railroad stop
32 The first or fifth letter of George
34 DeMille films
35 Overly
36 Simulate, as an old battle
39 "Where ___?"
42 Goethe classic
43 Early evening hour
45 1998 Sandra Bullock film
50 Bronx Bomber
51 Comfortable with
52 Life of Riley
54 Parts of bridles
55 Words that can precede the starts of 20-, 29- and 45-Across
61 Grand ___ (wine words)
62 Mob scenes
63 Column style
64 Feel sick
65 Gas in a layer

66 Flash of light
67 Free TV sport: Abbr.
68 Obsolete VCR's
69 Brief brawl

DOWN

1 [sigh]
2 Closet invader
3 Taj Mahal site
4 Cafeteria headwear
5 Adder, e.g.
6 Williams of tennis
7 Hint
8 "___ it the truth!"
9 Pitiful
10 Tricky curve
11 Dissident Sakharov
12 Mackerellike fish
13 Rise and shine
21 Wrecker's job

22 Young newts
25 What Sgt. Friday sought
26 It's not breaking the sound barrier anymore
27 London facility
28 ET's ride
30 Busybody
31 Place for sweaters?
33 Transplant, of a sort
37 Praise posthumously
38 "___ Beso" (1962 hit)
39 Gardner of Hollywood
40 Stag attendees
41 Sign, as a deal
42 A.T.F. agents, e.g.
44 Mask opening

45 Lug nuts' cover
46 Husband of Isis
47 "Downtown" singer Clark
48 Acts the coquette
49 Used a bench
53 Drinks from a flask
56 Radish or carrot
57 European erupter
58 "What's ___ for me?"
59 Salon job
60 Prefix with plasm
62 Stick up

by Nancy Kavanaugh

ACROSS

1 Tackle's protection
5 Indian silk center
10 Letters for a religious scholar
13 Outlet output: Abbr.
14 Funny cars might burn it
15 Curb, with "in"
17 Sports car, familiarly
18 More blue?
19 "Argghh!"
20 What fall traditionally brings
23 Intoxicating
24 Restaurant posting
25 Part of a school's Web site name
26 Shore soarer
27 "Sprechen ___ Deutsch?"
30 Annie or Dondi, of the comics
32 Collectors' goals
34 Hydrocarbon suffixes
37 Staff members: Abbr.
38 Ones responding to 20-Across
41 "Git!"
44 Mess overseers: Abbr.
45 Bounders
49 Easy marks
51 Old White House inits.
53 "Nope"
54 Suffix with human
55 Luxury
58 Screwball
60 What 38-Across might take
64 Sportswear brand
65 Shot from a tee

66 Word before and after "à"
67 Back-to-school mo.
68 Like some shoes and drinks
69 Actresses Balin and Claire
70 1965 Ursula Andress film
71 ___ nous
72 Cig. boxes

DOWN

1 Beauties
2 "None missing"
3 Not giving in one bit
4 Throw hot water on
5 Pro's foe
6 "Your majesty"
7 Drang's counterpart
8 Am I, doubled
9 Rita of "West Side Story"
10 Track race
11 Sly laughs
12 Patronized, as a restaurant
16 One result of a perfect game
21 Fleur-de-___
22 Presences
28 It makes "adverb" an adjective
29 Cuts off
31 Infinitesimal division of a min.
33 Did laps, say
35 Grade A item
36 Clockmaker Thomas
39 Louvre pyramid architect

40 Tilde's shape, loosely
41 Pooh-poohs
42 Spicy ingredients
43 Leader in a holiday song
46 As old as the hills
47 Upper Midwesterner
48 Social problem
50 Sit on it
52 Pan Am competitor
56 S. C. Johnson wrap
57 Boot
59 Cobwebby area
61 Monitor's measure
62 Assert
63 Turn over

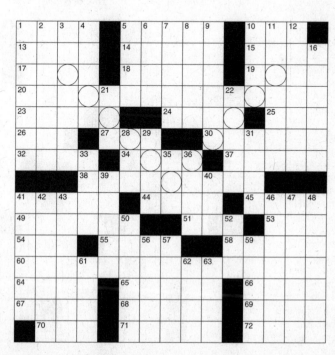

by Patrick Merrell

ACROSS

1 How ham may be served in a sandwich
6 Popular kitchen wrap
11 Tiny bit, as of hair cream
14 Oscar Mayer product
15 Skip to the altar
16 Bill Joel's "___ to Extremes"
17 The Bard
19 Judges administer it
20 Hammed it up
21 Thick urban air condition
23 City where "Ulysses" is set
26 Item carried by a dog walker
28 Columbus sch.
29 "Mona Lisa" features that "follow" the viewer
32 Years, to Cicero
33 Large bays
35 PIN points
37 Concept
40 Shopping ___
41 Theme of this puzzle
42 Shopping ___
43 ___ Romeo (Italian car)
44 G.M. car
45 Birth-related
46 Ancient South American
48 Meditative exercises
50 Spanish "that"
51 Lions and tigers and bears
54 Stage comments to the audience
56 Alternative
57 Safes
60 Turncoat
61 Very scary
66 Spanish cheer
67 Synthetic fiber
68 Continental money
69 Neither's partner
70 Mexican money
71 Gaucho's rope

DOWN

1 Delivery room docs, for short
2 "I don't think so"
3 Major TV brand
4 Bumpkin
5 Foes
6 Equinox mo.
7 Out of the wind, at sea
8 All of them lead to Rome, they say
9 Tax mo.
10 Liam of "Schindler's List"
11 Rundown
12 Staring
13 Shady garden spot
18 Major TV brand
22 One of the friends on "Friends"
23 Bedrock belief
24 Commonplace
25 Waver of a red cape
27 Throw, as dice
30 Count's counterpart
31 Pore over
34 Projecting rim on a pipe
36 Japanese soup
38 Wipe out
39 World book
41 Pillow filler
45 Not as nice
47 Drive-in restaurant server
49 Grand party
51 Element with the symbol B
52 Author Calvino
53 Lesser of two ___
55 It's debatable
58 Suffix with buck
59 Big coffee holders
62 With 64-Down, reply to "Am too!"
63 Tax adviser's recommendations, for short
64 See 62-Down
65 Fed. property overseer

by Steve Kahn

ACROSS

1 Fall (over)
5 Stadium walkways
10 At a distance
14 Wall Street letters
15 10 out of 10, e.g.
16 Western tie
17 Gambling actor?
19 Savvy about
20 Most miniature
21 Waiting room sound, maybe
22 Aloof
23 Keep ___ (persist)
25 Queue before Q
28 Gambling baseballer?
34 Pile up
36 Hydrox alternative
37 Avoiding the draft?
38 "___ Ha'i"
39 Hardhearted
40 Mrs. Dithers, in "Blondie"
41 Getting ___ years
42 Have dog breath?
43 Jerry or Jerry Lee
44 Gambling singer?
47 Take-home
48 "Queen for ___" (old TV show)
49 "Go ahead, shoot!"
51 Muscat, for one
54 Tallinn native
59 Anise-flavored liqueur
60 Gambling senator?
62 Stink
63 Hearing-related
64 Teetotalers' org.
65 Campbell of "Party of Five"
66 Feel blindly
67 Cold-shoulder

DOWN

1 Shoelace problem
2 Brontë heroine
3 In ___ (actually)
4 Téa of film
5 Steakhouse offering
6 Sidewalk stand beverages
7 5-Down, e.g.
8 Follow with a camera
9 ___-mo
10 180° turn
11 Henry Winkler role, with "the"
12 Sask. neighbor
13 Piece next to a knight
18 Barbershop boo-boos
21 1,002, in old Rome
23 Some of them are secret
24 "Iliad" locale
25 Fat cat
26 Muscat native
27 Michael of "Monty Python"
29 ___ public
30 Maine college town
31 Taken wing
32 Bone-chilling
33 You'll get a rise out of it
35 Asian city-state
39 Humane grp.
43 Popular disinfectant
45 Work of praise
46 Fight it out
50 Has memorized
51 "Tell me more"
52 Like some awakenings
53 Sea of ___ (Black Sea arm)
54 Eliel's architect son
55 Quick pic
56 Cast wearer's problem
57 Westernmost Aleutian
58 It may be proper
60 What "it" plays
61 Capek play

by Adam Cohen

ACROSS

1 Itch site
6 Athos, Porthos and Aramis
10 With 69-Across, caped crusader player of 1966
14 Spinners' output
15 Like water under the bridge
16 Palm starch
17 Koran focus
18 Sight from a fjord
19 ___ Hubbard
20 Caped crusader player of 1989
23 Fed. watchdog
24 Fabric rib
25 Excellent
28 Bitter end?
30 Fizz producer
32 Spanish carnival
33 Butler of fiction
35 Order
37 Elbow-bender
38 Caped crusader player of 1995
41 Space station name
44 Kite part
45 Nancy of "Access Hollywood"
48 Show flexibility
50 Part of A.C.L.U.: Abbr.
52 Catty call
54 1:51, 2:51 or 3:51, e.g.
56 Put-on
58 Bruin who wore a 4
59 Caped crusader player of 1997
62 Rude response
64 Old times
65 Of service
66 Razor name
67 School for Prince William
68 Pitches
69 See 10-Across

70 Sunset shade
71 "Now you ___, now . . ."

DOWN

1 Flower part
2 Item with adjustable legs
3 Not involving check or credit
4 Wife of Jacob
5 "Ridiculous!"
6 God who killed the dragon Python at Delphi
7 27- and 41-Down, and others
8 Molokai, for one
9 Greek porticos
10 Slanting
11 Hole fixers
12 Give it ___
13 Fall football night: Abbr.

21 It's between Long Bch. and Pasadena
22 Sporting plumage
26 "Flying Down to ___"
27 With 41-Down, this puzzle's theme
29 A few: Abbr.
31 Feel low
34 Needle work?
36 Not worried about right and wrong
39 Sportage maker
40 "Shiny Happy People" band, 1991
41 See 27-Down
42 Despot Amin
43 Park sightings
46 Strong and proud

47 Rhine temptress
49 Intently view
51 Epoch of the Tertiary period
53 Most bitterly amusing
55 Doughnut shop fixture
57 Deletions
60 Head for
61 Native Nebraskan
62 Talking point?
63 Three months abroad

By Elizabeth C. Gorski

ACROSS

1 "So long!"
5 Burden
9 Museo in Madrid
14 Death notice
15 It follows song or slug
16 Pine exudation
17 Gets together in person
20 "Blondie" or "Beetle Bailey"
21 Tennis champ Steffi
22 Vegetable that rolls
23 Narrow street
26 Jannings of old movies
28 Confronts, with "with"
34 "___ Baba and the 40 Thieves"
35 "Kiss me" miss
36 Tangle
37 Dietary no-no for Mrs. Sprat
39 Holds on to
42 Tiny weight
43 Former Argentine dictator
45 Actress Patricia of "The Subject Was Roses"
47 Drunkard's woe, for short
48 Returns a gaze
52 Ugandan tyrant Idi ___
53 Rules, shortly
54 Pres. Lincoln
57 Urges (on)
59 "Gesundheit!" preceder
63 Strolls, as with a sweetheart
67 1950's candidate Stevenson
68 B or B+, say
69 Nobelist Wiesel
70 Irish poet who wrote "The Lake Isle of Innisfree"
71 Lambs' mothers
72 Soaks

DOWN

1 Big gobblers
2 Aid and ___
3 Layer
4 Famous Hun
5 Not at work
6 Teachers' org.
7 Grp. that patrols shores
8 Sound system
9 Opposite of losses
10 Ump
11 "Quickly!"
12 Backgammon equipment
13 Prime draft status
18 Not spare the rod
19 Domesticate
24 Bismarck's state: Abbr.
25 Toward sunrise, in Mexico
27 Yearn (for)
28 Precipitation at about 32°
29 Crown
30 Itsy-bitsy
31 Late
32 Speak from a soapbox
33 Stately shade trees
34 Austrian peaks
38 Comic Dunn formerly of "S.N.L."
40 Person of equal rank
41 Fill up
44 Unbeatable foe
46 Boston airport
49 ['Tis a pity!]
50 Capture, as one's attention
51 Shun
54 Not home
55 Requested
56 Fitzgerald, the First Lady of Jazz
58 Precipitation below 32°
60 Robust
61 "Don't bet ___!"
62 Lyric verses
64 Krazy ___
65 Mother deer
66 They're checked at checkpoints, in brief

by Kurt Mengel and Jan-Michele Gianette

ACROSS

1 "Hold on there!"
5 Tiled art
11 Suffix with glob
14 Help for the stumped
15 Not rejecting out of hand
16 Stetson, for one
17 Particular
18 Nonsense
20 Fun time, slangily
21 Does superbly, as a stand-up comic
22 The March King
23 1988 Olympics site
25 L'Oreal competitor
26 Nonsense
30 ___ left field
31 Cast-of-thousands films
32 It may be 20%
35 Iowa State city
36 Zoo behemoth
37 Dairy Queen order
38 It begins in Mar.
39 Handed out
40 Knight stick?
41 Nonsense
43 Book boo-boos
46 Latish bedtime
47 Ready to fall out, as pages from a book
48 60's "V" sign
51 Relax, with "out"
53 Nonsense
55 Chess player's cry
56 Conditions
57 Crater Lake's state
58 Composer ___ Carlo Menotti
59 Bottom line
60 "Maybe later"
61 1070, in old Rome

DOWN

1 Taylor or Tyler, politically
2 Go 0-for-20, say
3 Bicycle or kayak, usually
4 20's dispenser
5 Alexander Calder creation
6 October birthstone
7 Broker's advice, at times
8 Added stipulations
9 Suffix in many ore names
10 Waist constrictors
11 Self-mover's rental
12 The end of one's rope?
13 Hawke of film
19 Hawk's opposite
21 Former baseball commissioner Bowie ___
24 Elevator pioneer
25 Puerto ___
26 Burlesque show props
27 Program for sobering up
28 Diner accident
29 Kunta ___ ("Roots" role)
32 In vain
33 Paycheck deduction
34 Have a look-see
36 C & W's McEntire
37 Lion tamer's workplace
39 Spoiled rotten, maybe
40 "Fatal Attraction" director Adrian
41 [I'm shocked!]
42 Museum guide
43 Like Santa's helpers
44 Pocahontas's husband
45 Cut of beef
48 Limerick writer, say
49 Fidgeting
50 Natural emollient
52 Boomers' kids
54 "___ y plata" (Montana's motto)
55 "The Wizard of Oz" studio

by Brendan Emmett Quigley

ACROSS

1 Prince before being kissed, in a fairy tale
5 Wooden-soled shoe
10 Suddenly asks
14 Terza ___ (Italian verse form)
15 Meeting place
16 Russian city on the Oka
17 ___ about (near)
18 General Mills brand
19 Flag
20 Eating Halloween-style?
23 Cameo gem
24 Kicks
25 Bovine advertising icon
29 Russian river
31 Halloween lunch fare?
35 Name
38 "Git out!"
39 Composer David famous for "Home on the Range"
40 Spanish "but"
41 Sun or moon
42 Halloween dinner fare?
44 Andean country
45 Arctic
46 Baltimore's ___ Museum
49 ___ were
52 Healthy Halloween dish?
58 Pro ___
59 Foreword
60 Kind of trip
62 Seine summers
63 Tangle
64 Bond foe
65 Arid
66 Vehicles carrying goods to market
67 Ruin

DOWN

1 To's partner
2 Symbol of constancy
3 Melville novel
4 Clothing
5 Audited, with "on"
6 Suffering
7 Wrinkle remover
8 Algerian port
9 Story
10 Large amount of stew
11 Stellar hunter
12 Candidate of 1992 and 1996
13 Flexible Flyers
21 Big name in movie theaters
22 Resorts
25 Cities Service competitor
26 Bert who sang "If I Were King of the Forest"
27 Social-climbing type
28 Altar avowal
29 "Whoops!"
30 Clinton's attorney general
32 Frankenstein's assistant, in film
33 Ballet wear
34 Smoke
35 Hand out
36 Constellation animal
37 Physicist Niels
40 Mideast grp.
42 Cad
43 ___ no good
44 "Pretty ___"
46 1990's Israeli P.M.
47 More than tickle
48 Ad photo caption
49 Showy flower
50 Diagonal spar
51 Dungeon sight
53 Money-related: Abbr.
54 Singer Paul
55 Pakistani language
56 Of two minds
57 Grit
61 ___-wop

by Nathaniel Weiss

ACROSS

1 Strait-laced
5 It can make you sick
9 Raise a glass to
14 Mrs. Chaplin
15 Charles Lamb's nom de plume
16 Stan's sidekick in old comedy
17 Gulf sultanate
18 After-bath powder
19 Mexican coins
20 "Get rid of your inhibitions!"
23 Phoned
24 Lennon's lady
25 Mil. stores
26 Hard ___ rock
28 Very, in Vichy
31 Indy racer sponsor
33 Baseball scores
35 Without much thought
37 Cuban line dance
41 "Dance the night away!"
44 Big mug
45 18-wheeler
46 Lacking slack
47 Sgt., for one
49 Easy marks
51 Mad Hatter's drink
52 Univ., e.g.
55 Downs' opposite
57 Hairdo
59 "Party hearty!"
65 Label with a name on it
66 Stench
67 Drop from the eye
68 Home of Arizona State

69 "___ my lips!"
70 Glowing review
71 Sauna feature
72 Concludes
73 Gave a thumbs-up

DOWN

1 Betting group
2 The Eternal City
3 Spellbound
4 Craze
5 "Control yourself!"
6 Israeli airline
7 Small stream
8 Very virile
9 A-one
10 Designer Cassini
11 Journalist Joseph
12 Language of the Omahas

13 Midterms, e.g.
21 Cable TV choice
22 Partner of a ques.
26 Synagogue chests
27 Office wear
29 "Grand" ice cream brand
30 Tart fruits
32 Frost or Burns
34 Where pores are
36 City WSW of Phoenix
38 Compulsive cleaner
39 Stickum
40 "The Thin Man" dog
42 Diamond in the rough, e.g.
43 Parachutists' lifelines

48 Select, with "for"
50 Female pig
52 Barbecue rods
53 West Pointer
54 Blackjack request
56 Seashell site
58 Foreword, for short
60 California wine valley
61 Steinbeck's "East of ___"
62 Little hopper
63 Roof's edge
64 ___ Scott decision, 1857

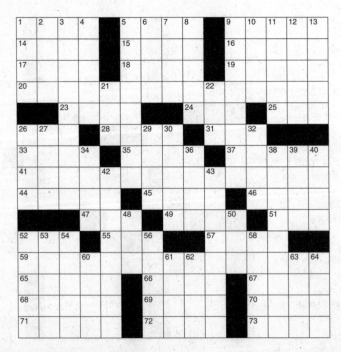

by Kendall Twigg and Nancy Salomon

ACROSS

1 Gangster's blade
5 Datebook entry: Abbr.
9 Brief news report
14 Prefix with -batic
15 Detective's discovery
16 Explode
17 Flying irritant
18 Runners
20 Pleasingly drawn
22 E.R. personnel
23 Tuscan home of St. Catherine
24 Last herb in a Simon & Garfunkel title
26 Clay, after 1964
29 Wildebeest
31 Cinderella's accompaniers to the ball
33 Caveat emptor phrase
36 Loll in a tub
38 Skewered food
39 Place for a bagel and a schmear
40 Binge
42 State bird of Hawaii
43 Area at a river's mouth
45 Having time on one's hands
46 Alum
47 Zoo baby
49 Islands welcome
51 Plastic ___ Band
52 Half of a 1960's pop quartet
54 Cattle breed
58 Bobby of hockey
59 Desperate final effort
61 Where elections are decided
65 Marc Antony's love, for short
66 Chemist Pasteur
67 Finished second
68 Château ___-Brion wine
69 Fathered
70 LAX listings: Abbr.
71 Wriggly biters

DOWN

1 Short stories they're not
2 Rousseau or Matisse
3 Furious
4 Booth, e.g.
5 Bank statement no.
6 Braid of hair
7 Obsolescent election item
8 A Kennedy
9 Rustic . . . and proud of it
10 Notable times
11 Scene-ending cry
12 Gibbon or orangutan
13 Scoreboard nos.
19 "___ la Douce"
21 ___ Gabriel
25 Rube
26 Yellow shade
27 Hotelier Helmsley
28 Under the covers
30 Beginning of many ship names
32 Potential problem with 7-Down
33 Enlarge, as one's lead
34 Greet, as a new year
35 Volunteer's statement
37 Kind of den
41 Long fish
44 It's often shared in theaters
48 Complain
50 Have a bite
53 Mexican restaurant bowlful
55 Inaugural balls
56 Deplete
57 Dalmatian features
58 Perennial battleground state
60 Retired Atl. fliers
61 Priestly garb
62 Bath water tester
63 Harbor craft
64 Grand ___ Opry

by Patrick Merrell

ACROSS

1 Infant's woe
6 Lux. neighbor
10 Hindu sacred text
14 Gene Tierney title role, 1944
15 Key next to *
16 King who abdicated in 1964
17 Perfumery supply
18 Nits, eventually
19 Big name in lithography
20 With 25-, 44- and 50-Across, Murphy's traffic law
23 Alliance of 1958–61: Abbr.
24 Our base system
25 See 20-Across
34 Type size
35 Touch
36 Pennsylvania, e.g.: Abbr.
37 Salt's direction
38 A Carpenter
40 Contractor's detail, for short
41 Lobbying org.
42 Vestments, e.g.
43 Dick's first second
44 See 20-Across
48 Brain scan, for short
49 Vane dir.
50 See 20-Across
58 34-Across alternative
59 Bookie's worry
60 Put forward
61 Abreast of
62 Kind of hygiene
63 Stage direction
64 Look after
65 Wind that can be piercing
66 Not just see

DOWN

1 Nail puller
2 Something to bleep, maybe
3 Cousin of a mandolin
4 It's south of Georgia
5 Paint the town red
6 Ravel classic
7 Cast-of-thousands
8 Polish hero Walesa
9 An absolute blast
10 Churchill gestures
11 Gutter locale
12 Annual bill
13 Web pop-ups, e.g.
21 Holman who was known as Mr. Basketball
22 Straight up
25 Sprang
26 Moor's deity
27 Reunion attendee
28 Time for les vacances
29 "Camille" star, 1937
30 U.K. award
31 Old wall covering
32 "If ___ Would Leave You"
33 Scout's mission
38 Pocket Books logo
39 "Odds ___ . . ."
40 Where to get soaked?
42 Celt, e.g.
43 Municipal vehicle
45 University founder ___ Stanford
46 Gauge part
47 Immigrant's subj.
50 Use a napkin
51 Desktop feature
52 Atkins no-no
53 "Ta-ta!"
54 Novelist Jaffe
55 Italian wine region
56 Score markings
57 Raison d'___
58 Wall Street order

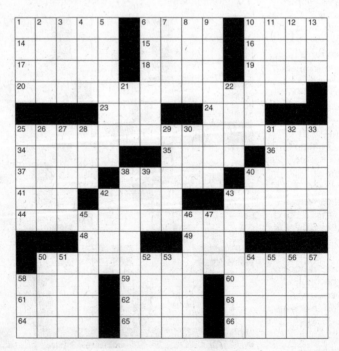

by Ed Early

ACROSS

1 Wildcat
5 "Hey . . . over here!"
9 Look without blinking
14 Smile proudly
15 Canyon sound
16 Artist's stand
17 Not crazy
18 Wander
19 The Little Mermaid
20 Pass along some football plays?
23 "The loneliest number"
24 Owl sound
25 Rots
29 Alexander ___, secretary of state under Reagan
30 Listening device
33 Texas battle site, with "the"
34 Does tailoring
35 McDonald's arches, e.g.
36 Begin to use wrestling feats?
39 Salt Lake City collegians
40 Sculls
41 Wall climbers
42 Club ___ (resort)
43 It turns at a pig roast
44 Dangerous African fly
45 Recipe direction
46 Tic-___-toe
47 Make time for aerobics classes?
54 Being from beyond Earth
55 Toward shelter
56 Not nerdy
58 Rain-snow mixture

59 Calendar span
60 Tackle box item
61 Jeans and khakis
62 Lushes
63 Side squared, for a square

DOWN

1 Dieters' units: Abbr.
2 "Right on!"
3 Mom's mom
4 Marvel Comics group
5 Eva and Juan
6 British biscuit
7 Old Iranian ruler
8 Weapons on the warpath
9 Veteran sailor
10 Cards for the clairvoyant

11 "Oh, that'll ever happen!"
12 Coral ridge
13 Building annexes
21 "___ want to dance?"
22 Cacophony
25 Informational unit
26 Overjoy
27 Like thick, dry mud
28 Iowa State's home
29 Valentine symbol
30 Namely
31 Moorehead of "Bewitched"
32 Sheriff's crew
34 Railing sites
35 Valentine subject
37 Stop by briefly

38 1970's-80's musical craze
43 Periods on jobs
44 "Any ___?"
45 Trapshooting
46 Pick up the tab
47 Winged stinger
48 Earthen pot
49 It means nothing to the French
50 Bread spread
51 Sch. where Bill Walton played
52 What a band may have planned
53 Achy
57 Meadow

by Damon J. Gulczynski

ACROSS

1 Cyber-junk mail
5 Nose-in-the-air type
9 "And thereby hangs ___"
14 To boot
15 Suffix with soft or china
16 Movado competitor
17 Jib or spanker
18 Eyebrow shape
19 Let up
20 Invoice surprises
23 Carol starter
24 Aussie jumper
25 Beanball target
28 One with answers
33 Guitarist Eddy
37 Antlers point
39 Comic Rudner
40 James Bond, e.g.
43 "___ Kampf"
44 Mimicker
45 Avian mimickers
46 To the rear
48 Slangy prefix meaning "mechanical"
50 Abbr. after an attorney's name
52 Buries
57 Hunter concealer
61 "Ulysses" author
63 Pupil controller
64 Captain of the Nautilus
65 "___ Day's Night" (Beatles film)
66 Demolish
67 Small combo
68 Miser's fixation
69 Airport postings, for short
70 "The ___ Baltimore" (Lanford Wilson play)

DOWN

1 Skater Cohen
2 Tartan pattern
3 Stage digression
4 Chocolatiers' equipment
5 "Old Folks at Home" river
6 Drug buster
7 Philharmonic grp.
8 Joy on "The View"
9 Catherine of ___
10 "Hamlet" soliloquy starter
11 "Sad to say . . ."
12 Court do-over
13 Program file extension
21 It'll knock you out
22 Al of "Today"
26 At the peak of
27 Navy Seal, e.g.
29 Bacchanalian blast
30 Austria's capital, to Austrians
31 Sicilian spouter
32 "Phooey!"
33 Russian legislature
34 French singles
35 Mine opening
36 Hawaii's state bird
38 Emperor who presided over a great fire
41 Reply to a childish taunt
42 In the company of
47 Pain reliever, e.g.
49 Skewed views
51 Paper purchase
53 Tither's amount
54 Month after diciembre
55 Send as payment
56 Barfly's seat
57 Printer's color
58 Plot measure
59 Beer bust locale
60 Four-time-wed Minnelli
61 Wing it, musically
62 Cry of revelation

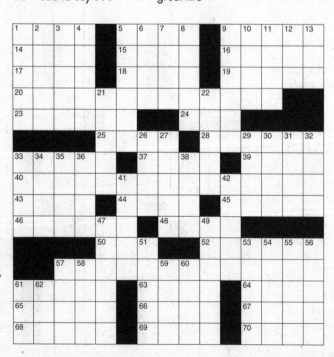

by Robert Dillman

ACROSS

1 Workplaces for some R.N.'s
4 It may be striped
8 Thin tufts
13 They beat the 39-Across in the 1986 8-Down
15 Old Modena family name
16 Actor Milo
17 Noodle concoction?
18 With 59-Across, 80+ year jinx that ended in 2004
20 Cookbook amts.
21 Donnybrook
22 "Entertaining Mr. ___" (Joe Orton play)
23 Spectral type
25 "It's my work, ___ say, and I do it for pay" (Dylan lyric)
26 Trains: Abbr.
27 Silvery gray
29 Perception
30 Roughly
32 Glasgow landowners
34 The National Pastime
38 Green-light
39 2004 jinx-breaking team, in headlines
40 Lover
41 2004 8-Down losers to the 39-Across, in headlines
43 Connects with
44 Zeno's home
45 Historic start?
46 Sound made with a frown
47 Avis offering
50 "Mighty ___ a Rose"
51 Literature Nobelist Hermann
53 Cream puff
55 Soccer ___
56 Circle parts
59 See 18-Across
61 Together, musically
62 Sphere
63 Hit man
64 59-Across, familiarly
65 Twisty turns
66 Infirmary count
67 Editor's backlog: Abbr.

DOWN

1 Exclude
2 They beat the 39-Across in the 1975 8-Down
3 Marriage acquisition, maybe
4 Sells down the river
5 Not on the briny
6 Hot pot
7 Jiffy
8 2004 event at which the jinx was broken
9 "And what ___ rare as a day in June?"
10 Cut
11 Showy flower
12 Hotel amenities
14 Cheek
19 Addicts
24 39-Across legend who played in the 1946 8-Down
25 Deception
27 Banned spray
28 Post-Christmas event
31 "O" in old radio lingo
33 Hotel amenity
34 39-Across, on scoreboards
35 Rijksmuseum locale
36 "I'm game"
37 Inspect, with "at"
39 Badlands Natl. Park's state
42 Give new weapons
43 Seismological activity
45 Buzzed
47 39+ inches, in Britain
48 Throbs
49 Court actions
52 Volvo rival
54 Skilled
55 Squeakers
57 8-Down also-rans to the 39-Across in 1918
58 Dates
60 Stain stopper

by David J. Kahn

ACROSS

1 Frozen treats
5 Soothing cream
9 Cursed
14 Chef's serving
15 Seller of his birthright, in Gen. 25
16 Hizzoner
17 ___'acte
18 Flexible, electrically
19 One with an amorous eye
20 Hidden advantage
23 "___ Doone" (romance)
24 Run-of-the-mill: Abbr.
25 Gentle ___ lamb
28 Lion, by tradition
33 Maybes
36 Den
37 Run for the ___ (Kentucky Derby)
38 Shingle site
40 Lady's title
43 Singer Horne
44 Farm measures
46 Dutch cheese
48 Yo-yo or Gobot
49 1950's–60's game show
53 Neighbor of Syr.
54 Second letter after epsilon
55 Dough leavener
59 Start of a nursery rhyme
63 Actress Kim
66 Hobbling
67 Israel's Abba
68 Nitrous ___ (laughing gas)
69 Shade trees
70 New Jersey hoopsters
71 Light sleeper
72 Affirmative votes
73 Understanding words

DOWN

1 Perfect
2 ___ de Mayo (Mexican holiday)
3 Fragrant compound
4 Psychiatrist, slangily
5 Regular drumming
6 Author Sholem
7 Put on board
8 Not quite all
9 Burn without a flame
10 What a worker earns
11 Popeye's Olive ___
12 Fish eggs
13 Mess up
21 It's on the tip of one's finger
22 Globe
25 Winning smile, they say
26 Dictation taker
27 Test mineralogically
29 "Platoon" setting
30 Actress Scala
31 Opposite of chaos
32 Netscape's owner
33 Baghdad resident
34 Concentrate
35 More achy
39 Lawyer's charge
41 Letters on a toothpaste tube
42 Irate
45 Athletic shoe
47 "___ help you?"
50 Agcy. that promotes fair competition
51 Markswoman Annie
52 Sana'a native
56 French clerics
57 List of candidates
58 Not relaxed
59 Green gem
60 Hay bundle
61 Jane Austen heroine
62 Loch ___
63 Sign of approval
64 Losing tic-tac-toe line
65 Namely: Abbr.

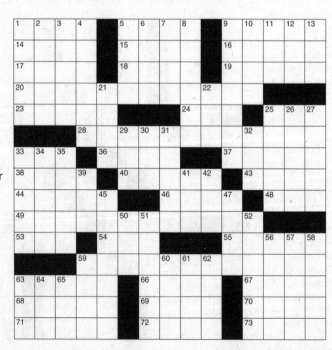

by Alison Donald

ACROSS

1 Rating a blue ribbon
5 Unceasingly
10 Sign over, as rights
14 Florence's river
15 Gossip's tidbit
16 W.W. II general Bradley
17 "Uh-uh!"
20 "The Natural" role Roy ___
21 Some parents
22 Sergeant once played by Phil Silvers
23 Unlocks, poetically
25 Doctor's charge
26 "Uh-uh!"
31 Mideast grp.
34 Higher on the Mohs scale
35 Basketball's ___ Ming
36 Words to an old chap
37 Fact-filled volume
39 Cultural programs they're not
41 Newshawk's source, often
42 Tacit approval
44 Food or air
45 Hook shape
46 "Uh-uh!"
48 "Now I see!"
49 Pro foe
50 "So long, mon ami"
53 Farmer's sci.
54 Mall stand
59 "Uh-uh!"
62 Bit attachment
63 Muralist Rivera
64 Within reason
65 Singer James or Jones
66 First name in cosmetics
67 Part of many "shoppe" names

DOWN

1 Sen. Evan of Indiana
2 Suffix with switch
3 Give the cold shoulder
4 Pyramid, maybe
5 "Chicago Hope" sets, for short
6 Pumpkin pie spice
7 Diplomat's post
8 Answers from a 49-Across
9 Hoopster Erving's nickname
10 Newswoman Roberts
11 Early Oscar winner ___ Jannings
12 Like a damp cellar
13 Hence
18 Ashe Stadium event
19 Outdated wedding-vow word
24 Voracious fish
25 One making arrangements
26 Jonah's swallower
27 Patriot Nathan and others
28 "Aunt ___ Cope Book"
29 Bismarck's state: Abbr.
30 ___ Tuesday (Mardi Gras)
31 "Nonsense!"
32 Andy Kaufman's role on "Taxi"
33 Yiddish "Egad!"
36 Analogist's words
38 Iowa college
40 Golf's Sorenstam
43 Where Friday was once seen on Thursday
46 Hoodlum
47 Cause to see red
48 Big name in health care
50 River of Bern
51 South Beach ___
52 "What's ___ for me?"
53 Black cuckoos
55 ___ facto
56 Fire ___ (gem)
57 E-mail command
58 Tot's perch
60 Lines from Shelley
61 Clod chopper

by Stella Daily and Bruce Venzke

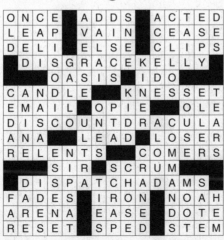

1

```
A B C S   B A L S A   O P T S
D A A E   I C E I N   B R I T
D I V A   C H A N D E L I E R
S T E W S   E S E   S A M O A
    A N D R E W   S T A N D
S E T T L E     R E E D
A S H E   A I S L E S   O S S
U S E R   L L O Y D   O N T O
L O P   P E L L E T   U N I T
    H E A R     A L T A R S
A D A I R   W E B B E R
G O N G S   I V E   N A G A T
O F T H E O P E R A   C A T S
R O O T   H E N R I   E R I K
A R M Y   O S T A R   D Y E S
```

2

```
  A P P A L   S E W N   A K A
P R E G O   C R E E   L A M
E I G H T E E N T W E L V E
K L M   A S I N   N U N N
R I M Y   O N E H U N D R E D
O K E E F F E   E R A S E R
C E S A R   G I G I
  T H I R T Y S E V E N
  D A R N   E W E R S
  B E S A M E   S U R E B E T
F I F T Y S E V E N   S U L U
A G F A   E L S E   L A B
T W O T H O U S A N D S I X
A I R   O A S T   A G A Z E
H G T   E K E S   P E T E R
```

3

```
P E S T   B U N K   A B B O T
E L I E   A R E A   S O R T S
N A T T U R N E R   T R I C K
S P U R N S   A M O R E
I S A A C   N E T P R O F I T
V E T   I L E N E S   W E R E
E S E   V E A L   B E R E T
  N I T P I C K E R
S E O U L   S H I N   V A R
A L A I   A T T I R E   E N E
N O T S O F A S T   A R R I D
  B A N T U   A T E A S E
E A R N S   N U T N H O N E Y
S P A C E   T R O T   I D E E
T E N E T   S I N E   L A D S
```

4

```
S E M I S   B E A U   C L E F
C A P R A   R O W S   L I N E
I T S A N Y O N E S G U E S S
        T O W   R U B O U T
W H O C A N S A Y   A C N E
R E P O   E L V I R A
I C E B A G   L E A D R O L E
S H R   B E A T S M E   C O N
T E A R I N T O   A D D E N D
  A G E O L D   I A G O
  F I C A   I D O N T K N O W
S A N K I N   U N O
C L U E L E S S R E P L I E S
A S S T   M A I L   A I S L E
B E E S   O P R Y   Z Z T O P
```

5

```
O N C E   A D D S   A C T E D
L E A P   V A I N   C E A S E
D E L I   E L S E   C L I P S
  D I S G R A C E K E L L Y
    O A S I S   I D O
C A N D L E   K N E S S E T
E M A I L   O P I E   O L E
D I S C O U N T D R A C U L A
A N A   L E A D   L O S E R
R E L E N T S   C O M E R S
    S I R   S C R U M
  D I S P A T C H A D A M S
F A D E S   I R O N   N O A H
A R E N A   E A S E   D O T E
R E S E T   S P E D   S T E M
```

6

7

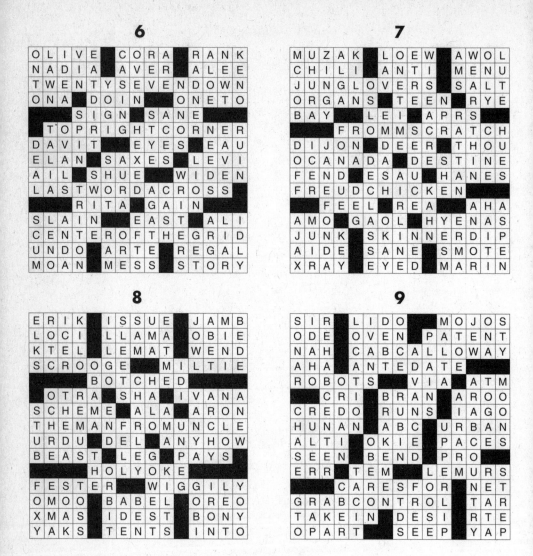

8

9

10

11

```
N E O N   O C H O   J O K E R
E L M O   O L A N   O D E T O
V I E W   H I S T   S E N A T
I O G A L L O N H A T S
S T A D I A   T E L L S A L L
    A R L O   D E A R I E
I O O Y E A R S W A R   D N A
P C T S   S H H   B E E P
A A H   I O O O I S L A N D S
S L E I G H   G O A D
S A R D O N I C   F I V E A M
    I O O O O M A N I A C S
S H Y O F   T R I B   B R E D
P E A C E   A A R E   E L I O
F L O Y D   S L E D   S Y N S
```

12

```
S P A S   N A S T   A R M S
E A M E S   U S E R   B E A T
T R U T H   D A T A   E B R O
  A N T I S E P T I C T A N K
U N D O N E   E T A   T E E
M O S   E D U C E   L E E R S
P I E   A A A   A I M
  A N T I T R U S T F U N D
  D O E   S A O   U R I
C R E S T   H E N N A   M I T
H E S   A P E   A S S E N T
A N T I S O C I A L W O R K
S T E P   S T O P   A B A S H
T A R S   S O N S   N I T T I
E L S E   E R S E   G E O M
```

13

```
W O N G   O M A R   W A G O N
E C O L   N I N E   A D E L E
E T U I   B R A N   L A T E X
D O N T Q U O T E M E   S S T
    C U T S   I S A W
S O W H A T   E S C A P I S M
A H A   S O O T H   E S A U
T A L K I N G T O M Y S E L F
A R N E   R A T I O   T E T
N E U R O S E S   L U G O S I
    T R A C   J A N N
T A C   T H E K I N G A N D I
A B A S E   B O N E   W O R D
P O K E R   B O G S   O V A L
E X E C S   S L O E   N A T E
```

14

```
M O B S   A R E A   C O D E S
A C R E   L U N G   R U I N S
S H E A   A L O E   O T T E R
H O W C O M E W R O N G
    O D O R   R E R E A D
I N A W E   S E N D   E N N E
N E L S O N   M A E   W A G S
S U B   N U M B E R S   M O I
O T I C   A B E   S H O E R S
L E N A   N A R C   E F L A T
E R O T I C   O L A F
    A R E N E V E R B U S Y
H A B L A   A L E E   E R T E
A F O O T   P E R K   A G U A
S T A G E   A C T S   T E N S
```

15

```
A T B A T   G O L F S   I C E
M O O L A   A W E E K   S O D
B R A I N F R E E Z E   O L D
E S T   G I R D S   T O S A Y
R O S E L L E   A C D C
    M E L T E D C H E E S E
W H A M S   A I R Y   L I D
R O B E   M A S S E   D E L I
A U S   S A L E   A I S L E
P R E T T Y P L E A S E
    N O R A   S C H M E A R
G O T T A   T O P I C   L S U
A P E   F L O R I D A K E Y S
Z E E   E A G L E   N O N E T
E L S   S T A Y S   S P A T S
```

16

```
M S N B C   R E I D   E W A N
U H A U L   E D N A   R A T E
C A N Y O U H E A R M E N O W
H M O   S P A N S   I N E P T
      A E O N   E N T O
T E S T I N G O N E T W O
A V I A N   I S A Y   R N A
M E N D   J A N E T   Z I O N
E R A   S O C K   B O N G O
    I S T H I S T H I N G O N
      T E N D   W A G E
C H A I N   T A I L S   A F T
H E L L O H E L L O H E L L O
A R A L   A S T I   O N E A M
D O N S   S T A T   T E X T S
```

17

```
W A V E   F A R M   M A R K S
A U E R   A R E A   I N A L L
X X X R A T I N G   R A D I O
      A R C   E N G A G I N G
S C O T I A   W A R C R I E S
P A P I S T S   I L A
O N I C E   A A A M E M B E R
R A N   B B B   R N A
E L E V E N E E E   A M A S S
      A X E   T A P E S U P
S T E N C I L S   R I N S E S
P E N D U L U M   A N D
A N D Y S   G E O R G E I I I
S T O K E   E L L A   R O A N
M O R E S   S T E T   S U N K
```

18

```
A S F A R   L S A T S   F I G
L A R G O   E P C O T   I R A
K I E R K E G A A R D   N O R
A N S E   T A R D E   D E N Y
    T H E A C T   I S N T
    S C H O P E N H A U E R
S M O T E   R O T E   N C O
H A L O   D R A N O   R E O S
A M Y   F I N N   S A D L Y
H A M M A R S K J O L D
    P E N T   E R R A T A
T W I N   P L A T S   R A R E
E R A   M O U S S O R G S K Y
R A D   G O A P E   O U T I E
M P S   T R U S T   O N E N D
```

19

```
M E N S A   A C A D   D I S C
P A N T S   L O G E   O B O E
S T E E P   E L I A   D I B S
      W I N K A N D R O S E S
A H A   R U E   E A S E I N
P A R K I N G F I N K   S T A
B R I A N   L O D E S
S P A M   C L A N S   A D A M
      A S H E N   P R I C E
S P A   L I N K O F S I G H T
A R T F U L   S R A   S E E
M A K E M I N E M I N K
I N I T   D E V O   D I N G Y
A C N E   O M E N   Q T I P S
M E S S   G O L D   S E P A L
```

20

```
T A S T E   S W A M P   T I L
A N T E S   P A N E L   O N E
B Y Y E S T E R D A Y   U T E
      E R A S   W A T E R
S P O O N E R   P R O U D L Y
H E N L E Y   C H O O S E
R A T E S   R O A L D   S U N
E C H O   P U R S E   T U N E
W E E   M E L E E   B R I D E
    D O O L E Y   L O O T E D
A M O U N T S   F I N D E R S
B O U T S   A L O E
O R B   T H I S I N S T A N T
M E L   E E R I E   U R I A H
B Y E   R E E F S   P A R T Y
```

21

B	R	A	S	S		S	T	E	N	O		S	A	P
E	A	T	U	P		P	I	N	E	A	P	P	L	E
A	R	O	M	A		E	N	T	E	R	T	A	I	N
R	E	P	O	R	T	C	A	R	D		E	R	A	S
			S	I	S	S	Y		P	R	E	S		
S	T	A	M	E	N		S	A	O					
L	O	V	E		C	O	R	K	E	R		P	E	W
A	A	A	A	A	A	A	A	A	A	A	A	A	A	A
M	T	S		I	N	T	E	N	T		L	I	V	Y
	D	R	S			T	R	A	D	E	S			
	A	L	E	S		S	C	A	L	A				
F	D	I	C		P	E	R	F	E	C	T	G	P	A
A	L	M	A	M	A	T	E	R		E	R	R	O	L
T	E	A	F	O	R	T	W	O		R	E	A	D	E
S	R	S		D	R	E	S	S		S	E	N	S	E

22

B	O	S	H		B	A	S	R	A		S	A	D	A
A	R	C	O		E	M	A	I	L		U	X	O	R
L	I	R	R		T	U	R	T	L	E	N	E	C	K
L	O	U	N	G	E	L	I	Z	A	R	D			
A	L	F		O	L	E	S			M	R	M	O	M
D	E	F	R	O	S	T		A	L	I	E	N	E	E
E	S	S	E			S	P	O	N	S	O	R	S	
		S	N	A	K	E	E	Y	E	S				
M	E	C	H	A	N	I	C			E	S	M	E	
D	E	P	O	N	E	D		B	R	I	S	T	O	L
S	N	O	U	T		A	E	O	N		R	O	E	
		L	E	A	P	F	R	O	G	G	I	N	G	
T	O	A	D	S	T	O	O	L	S		A	P	I	A
A	N	N	E		M	E	R	I	T		P	E	E	N
G	E	A	R		O	M	E	N	S		E	R	S	T

23

B	A	S	H		C	A	B	S		A	D	H	O	C
E	L	I	A		O	R	E	O		D	R	A	W	S
D	E	L	I		F	R	E	D		D	O	N	N	A
S	E	L	L	S	F	O	R	A	S	O	N	G		
			S	L	E	W		U	N	E	A	S	Y	
	A	R	T	I	E		A	P	E	S		R	O	I
S	W	O	O	N		A	R	I	D		S	O	U	P
C	H	A	N	G	E	S	O	N	E	S	T	U	N	E
R	I	D	E		L	A	S	T		W	A	N	D	S
A	R	T		D	U	P	E		W	A	R	D	S	
P	L	O	W	E	D			P	E	R	T			
	F	A	C	E	S	T	H	E	M	U	S	I	C	
C	R	A	V	E		H	O	O	D		R	U	S	H
H	E	M	E	N		A	N	N	E		N	I	L	E
E	X	E	R	T		D	Y	E	D		S	T	E	W

24

C	B	S		C	R	O	C		M	A	L	A	W	I
R	E	A		H	A	L	L		E	D	I	T	E	D
I	C	U		U	S	D	A		S	H	A	M	E	S
N	O	N	E	T	H	E	W	I	S	E	R			
G	O	A	T	E	E		C	U	R		S	E	W	
E	L	S	A		S	O	M	E	P	E	O	P	L	E
			A	T	N	O		S	N	E	A	K	S	
A	I	M	E	R		A	I	L		T	R	Y	S	T
C	R	I	S	C	O		S	E	E	S				
M	O	S	T	W	A	N	T	E	D		D	U	A	L
E	N	T		E	R	A			U	G	A	N	D	A
			A	L	L	Y	O	U	C	A	N	E	A	T
U	P	S	I	D	E		G	N	A	T		A	G	E
S	T	A	R	E	S		L	I	T	E		S	E	N
S	A	T	Y	R	S		E	X	E	S		E	S	S

25

M	A	H	I		P	A	L	E	S		B	A	T	S
A	S	I	F		O	F	A	R	T		E	D	I	E
B	I	G	F	A	T	L	Y	R	E		A	L	A	P
		H	I	D			L	O	N		M	I	R	A
	C	H	E	M	I	C	A	L	C	Y	M	B	A	L
F	L	O	R	I	D	A		H	E	E				
O	A	R		T	O	R	C	H		A	U	D	I	S
R	I	S	E		S	T	R	U	M		P	E	N	A
E	M	E	N	D		A	T	B	A	T		C	D	I
			T	O	M			B	R	O	I	L	E	D
Q	U	A	R	T	E	R	B	A	C	K	S	A	X	
U	N	C	A		N	E	O			E	A	R		
A	S	O	N		S	T	O	L	E	N	B	A	S	S
D	A	R	C		C	R	E	O	N		E	N	T	O
S	Y	N	E		H	O	D	A	D		L	T	R	S

26

```
R O C K   I N L E T   A B L E
U G L I   B O O T H   S L U G
B R O N Z E S T A R   T U N A
Y E T   E R E   L I P R E A D
      M L I     L E A R
P A G O D A S   S L A Y I N G
I L O N A   M I T E R   B O L
P O L K   F A D E D   A B O U
E N D   A A R O N   S H O N E
D E M E R I T   O C T A N E S
    E M I R     O R B
R E D C A P S   D R U   P S I
A L A E   L O V I N G C U P S
M I L E   A D O R E   O P A L
P A S S   Y A W E D   Z A N E
```

27

```
A I N T   P L E A   A D M A N
S N O O T I E S T   R A I S E
T H E K I N G S T O N T R I O
R E V E L S       P I E
I R I S   S P R E E   A R T
D E L   P E A L E D   A C I D
    C A T N A P   E T H O S
  T H E R A J Q U A R T E T
F R O N T   O U T M A N
E A S T   I S E E I T   N I A
E Y E   A M E S S   G E N S
    E I N     D R E A D S
T H E T R O U T Q U I N T E T
W A S T E   R A R E B R E E D
A L T A R   N E S T   E R D A
```

28

```
F E T E   A B O V E   A M A T
U L A N   C U B I T   V A R Y
J A C Q U E L I N E   I R O N
I L I U M   K E Y   S A L M A
    T I P     L A O T I A N
H O U R   I N D   M O O N S
A W R Y   B O U V I E R
L E N   K E N N E D Y   S T U
  O N A S S I S   H M O S
  R O R E M   T N T   E O N S
S A D D E S T     S L O
A I D E S   W P A   R I T T S
U S M A   P I L L B O X H A T
D I A L   O X I D E   E L S A
I N N S   S T E A L   S Y S T
```

29

```
S T O R E   E S A U   S O A R
T R A I L   C H I N   Y U L E
O U T O F D O O R S   R T E S
W E S T   O N R Y E   I O T A
    E P C O T   N O N F A T
P O O D L E   L E T S G O
E M U   E N C Y C   M E R C I
R A T   A T A   R I O   D A D
T R O T S   P O U T S   E R E
    F E E D E R   S I E R R A
I M P E D E   B L E S S
T A R P   S T I L L   P A C S
E R I E   O U T O F S I G H T
M I N E   T R E S   E E R I E
S O T S   O K R A   A D A P T
```

30

```
S A H I B   O P E R A   B A R
A M I N O   W A L T S   O N O
P I C K Y P I C K E T   N I B
      C E N T S   A U N T Y
R A P S O N G S   L I B Y A N
E R U P T S   C A R I B
S T P A T   B O O Z E   O O F
T O P S   S A R G E   E N T R
S O Y   B A R B S   P E N T A
      P U L S E   H I R E O N
T A U R U S   A N A L Y T I C
A P P L E   E R O D E
L A P   J U N K Y J U N K E T
I R E   A N G I E   P I A N O
A T T   Y A R N S   S A N D Y
```

31

```
D O B R O   T R O D   Z A P S
I S L E T   R O L E   A M I E
P L A N E   O P E C   G I L L
S O H E L P M E G O D   N O M
    G L O P     D A K O T A
W E R E O V E R H E R E
A L I       E A S I N E S S
I L O V E   A N T   N O L I E
L A T I T U D E       I L L
    T H R O W T H E B A L L
M O S A I C     A U E R
O U I   C H E C K P L E A S E
R I T A   I R A E   I N I N K
A J A R   N O T I   E D D I E
L A R K   S O O N   R A S P S
```

32

```
W A L K S   A B E L   N A T S
I N E R T   C L I O   I N I T
S T E A L   C A N O P E N E R
P I C K U P T H E P A C E
    S H A K E S     L E M O N
    T E N   B A W L   E R E
E S S O   S E R G E I   A B S
P U T A F I R E U N D E R I T
S I R   R O D E N T   V A T S
O T O   O N E D   A L I
M E N D S     A P O L L O
    G E T T H E L E A D O U T
C U B B Y H O L E   T O R T E
S P O T   O M A R   H E A R S
I N X S   R E N T   E R N E S
```

33

```
O A H U   G O O P   D A R N S
O L A N   A C R E   E L I O T
M I D D L E E A R   P L A T A
P B S   A L A N   L O O S E N
H I T C H I N G P O S T
    L O C   L Y E S O A P
A D E E R   S H E A   M N O
C O F F E E T A B L E B O O K
E S T   L A T E   L O O N Y
D E S P A I R     A D S
    E N T R A N C E H A L L
M I L L I E   T E C S   W O O
A R I L S   F R E E T R A D E
R A R E E   A I D S   O R E S
K E A T S   B A S S   T E N S
```

34

```
G S A   P A S T S   A D L E R
O H S   O C T A L   M I A T A
B I P   D H A B I   P S Y C H
A R C H I E B U N K E R
D R A M A   G I R A F F E
    S T O O P   P E E R I N
A B U   R O D E O   L A N A
B E T T Y F O R D C L I N I C
A T I E   M O O L A   C S T
C O L L I E   T R I B E
K N E E C A P   R E G A L
    V E R O N I C A L A K E
A D L I B   G O M A D   V I N
L A S S O   O R O N O   E T O
I N D E X   S A N E R   L A X
```

35

```
T A R O   A S T A   B A B A S
O D O R   D A I S   A M I G O
N A S A   O M N I   Y O D E L
S M A L L P O T A T O E S
    A T A   H U B
A W A R D S   T O E   A S S T
C O N E D   M A N I A   H I E
T R I V I A L P U R S U I T S
O R S   E R I E S   S P R A T
R Y E S   G I S   R I S E R S
    T O O   A E S
    P E T T Y O F F I C E R S
A D U L T   A N T E   A V O W
T U L L E   L E E R   L I M A
M O L A R   E R R S   F L A T
```

36

```
E R I C ■ L I L A C ■ A M E N
D A D O ■ A B O I L ■ P I L E
T H O M A S M O R E ■ A S I S
■ ■ B U T S ■ ■ A O R T A S ■
O B L I G E ■ D O N A T E ■ ■
L E A N E D ■ R U S T ■ R T E
D A T E R ■ M A T E S ■ C E L
I T I S ■ J A P E S ■ C H A D
E E N ■ H U G E R ■ R A I S E
S N L ■ A M O R ■ H A R P E R
■ O L D B O Y ■ O D I S T S
N A V A J O ■ A R I L ■ ■
A L E C ■ J O H N M I L T O N
S E R E ■ E L A T E ■ O K I E
H E S S ■ T A M I L ■ N O L O
```

37

```
N A R C ■ M I L E ■ B A I T S
A D I A ■ A M E S ■ A P N E A
B O G [USA] L I B I S ■ S L A N G
■ A L I N E ■ O H S [USA] N N A
A F T ■ A M A J ■ D O V E I N
C O O L ■ A T E S T ■ E R S
T U N E I N ■ R O V E R ■ ■
I L I A D ■ [USA][USA][USA] ■ P A W N S
■ ■ V I G I L ■ T A G O U T
S S E ■ A R E A S ■ E R L E
T H O [USA] N D ■ M R E D ■ K L M
R E C L U S E ■ O L I O S ■
A R I O T ■ Y O [USA] I D W H A T
S P A N S ■ R E L O ■ L O P E
H A L E Y ■ E R S T ■ S P E D
```

38

```
B E E C H ■ S A L T ■ I S A K
A D L A I ■ O R E O ■ A C R E
Y U M M Y Y U M M Y ■ G R A D
■ ■ P A A R ■ ■ S C R U B S
A C T S ■ N O D S ■ H E M S
T H A I ■ K N E E D E E P ■
R U S T S ■ S T Y E ■ T I A
I N T E A R S ■ H E R O I N E
A G E ■ H A H A ■ S N O U T
■ S T A G E M O M ■ T U R N
■ A G A R ■ A S I A ■ A S E A
A O R T A S ■ L A I R ■ ■
G L E E ■ M M M M M M G O O D
R E A R ■ O B O E ■ P E D R O
A R T S ■ G A I N ■ S T E E R
```

39

```
E A G L E ■ C A M P ■ R A N K
M O R O N ■ A W O L ■ O D I E
B R A N D O N A M E ■ M A N Y
E T S ■ G R E Y ■ T H A M E S
R A S C A L S ■ S H I N ■ ■
■ ■ A M Y ■ P H O T O O P S
P A S T E ■ H A I R ■ F L A T
A U T O ■ B E R R A ■ O G L E
C R A B ■ E A S T ■ G R A S P
T A B U L A T E ■ S O U ■ ■
■ ■ R I C H ■ C L A M S U P
L E N G T H ■ G O A L ■ P R O
I D O L ■ B O N O V O Y A G E
A G R A ■ U R A L ■ N O T E S
R E A R ■ M E W S ■ G U S S Y
```

40

```
C O R E A ■ S T A T ■ S K I N
O R A L S ■ L I V E ■ L A N E
N I P A T ■ I D E A ■ O N T O
J O I N I N M A R R I A G E ■
O L E ■ ■ E E L ■ ■ S N A R L
B E R A T E S ■ A F T ■ R I O
■ ■ L A D ■ O D E ■ W O O F
W E W O U L D F O R S H O R T
E X I T ■ E A T ■ T I E ■ ■
L P S ■ D D S ■ D I R E C T S
L E T M E ■ ■ P A L ■ A H A
■ D A Y B E F O R E T H U R S
E I R E ■ T A L K ■ O A S I S
S T I R ■ N I K E ■ A L E V E
S E A S ■ A L A N ■ D O S E D
```

41

```
HAUL . IRISH . CHIA
ASTA . TABOO . LOON
STICKSHIFT . UPTO
NICELY . ARABIAN
TRADE . ACROSS .
. ECRU . DIONNE
LIMB HOES . ADIOS
ARIA . OSCAR . ATIT
RANTS . EAST . SERE
ANIMAL . RHEA .
. ONEIDA . CREME
SOYBEAN . SNARES
ALAI . PADDLEBOAT
GIRL . ENTRE . IDLE
ANNE . RESEW . NESS
```

42

```
FOAL . CUBS . ONSET
OMNI . ASAP . VERNE
LETO . MERE . ERODE
KNITTEDSCARF .
. TIL . SCH . THO
COCACOLA . HEAROF
ALL . TIMBERWOLF
REEFS . MBA . ELUDE
BARRELBOLT . PER
ORIOLE . YIELDERS
NYC . EAR . EAU .
. INHALINGFOOD
HINDI . JENA . FOUR
ADIEU . AGOG . EZRA
SALEM . HONE . LEST
```

43

```
INLAW . ALFA . POLE
NOOSE . BORE . RHEA
FELTINONESBONES
OLLA . EDGE . IVORY
. ROHE . LUKE .
JUSTDISCOVERED
OSTEO . AVE . BRED
HUA . MACLEAN . ATE
NATS . RAE . EPSOM
. LETTERBEFOREXI
. RASP . LINO .
STRAW . ODIN . POPS
CROSSWORDSTAPLE
AILS . ELIE . ONEAL
MOLE . TSPS . MESTA
```

44

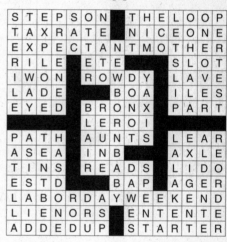

```
STEPSON . THELOOP
TAXRATE . NICEONE
EXPECTANTMOTHER
RILE . ETE . SLOT
IWON . ROWDY . LAVE
LADE . BOA . ILES
EYED . BRONX . PART
. LEROI .
PATH AUNTS . LEAR
ASEA . INB . AXLE
TINS . READS . LIDO
ESTD . BAP . AGER
LABORDAYWEEKEND
LIENORS . ENTENTE
ADDEDUP . STARTER
```

45

```
SONIC . HOLM . IRES
ERICH . ERIE . NOAH
WAKEISLAND . NAVE
ORE . SCI . TAPERED
NESTEA . TYLER .
. ELLER . SOCKET
DOWN . DRAW . NINAS
IRON . SOFAS . ROSA
SCRIP . OFAN . CBER
KANSAS . ICALL .
. CYNIC . PAELLA
DEPOSIT . OAR . AIM
ESAU . PAWNTICKET
STIR . ELEE . ARENO
KENT . RYES . TORSO
```

46

O	N	A	N		B	I	N	G		B	Y	F	A	R
N	O	M	O		I	S	E	E		E	A	R	L	Y
A	L	I	T		G	A	R	R		S	M	O	T	E
I	T	S	N	O	T	Y	O	U	I	T	S	M	E	
R	E	S	O	L	E			N	O	B				
			W	E	N	E	E	D	T	O	T	A	L	K
L	P	S		S	T	A	G		A	Y	E	A	Y	E
E	R	O	S		R	A	G		E	R	L	E		
N	O	F	U	S	S		D	A	M	N		P	E	P
I	W	A	N	T	M	Y	S	P	A	C	E			
			D	O	A		D	A	L	L	A	S		
	W	E	V	E	G	R	O	W	N	A	P	A	R	T
B	A	C	O	N		R	H	E	E		A	C	N	E
E	C	O	L	I		O	N	E	S		S	E	A	N
D	O	N	T	S		W	O	K	S		O	R	Z	O

47

P	L	O	P			N	C	O			A	P	P	L	E
R	I	P	A		K	O	O	L		G	L	E	A	M
E	S	A	U		L	E	A	D		R	E	L	I	T
P	A	L	L	M	A	L	L		Z	E	A	L		
			V	A	T	S		L	E	E		G	T	O
R	A	P	I	D	S		A	N	D	I	R	O	N	
E	M	I		A	C	T	O	R			R	A	M	S
P	O	L	L	T	H	E	A	U	D	I	E	N	C	E
E	E	L	S		S	T	E	A	D		T	A	T	
A	B	O	U	N	D	S			B	E	A	S	T	S
L	A	W		A	A	A		T	B	A	R			
			T	R	I	M		P	U	L	L	O	V	E	R
A	V	A	I	L		N	U	D	E		M	A	Y	O
W	I	L	D	E		I	Z	O	D		A	M	E	X
L	A	K	E	R		T	O	R			S	P	R	Y

48

P	E	Z		E	D	G	Y		P	O	W	W	O	W
E	C	O		T	A	L	E		I	D	O	I	D	O
C	H	O	W	C	H	O	W		T	E	R	R	O	R
S	O	S	A		L	A	S	S		S	E	R	F	
		C	H	I	T		E	L	S	E				
	T	A	K	E	A	S	O	L	E	M	N	V	O	W
B	O	S	O	X		W	I	N	E		A	N	A	
A	R	K		A	M	O	N	G	S	T		S	L	R
T	S	E		G	O	R	E			A	S	C	O	T
H	O	W	N	O	W	B	R	O	W	N	C	O	W	
			A	N	N	E		B	E	A	R			
M	A	I	M		D	A	L	I		U	F	O	S	
A	S	S	E	S	S		H	I	G	H	B	R	O	W
S	T	A	I	R	S		A	G	H	A		E	P	A
K	O	W	T	O	W		B	E	T	H		E	S	P

49

C	R	I	S	P		D	A	H	L		T	A	D	S
S	A	N	T	A		A	R	E	A		O	R	E	L
A	N	T	E	C	E	D	E	N	T		W	I	L	E
			H	E	S	T	O	N		E	M	I	G	R	E
O	P	E	D		D	E	A	L	W	I	T	H	I	T
O	A	T		L	S	D		V	O	N		T	O	Y
P	L	U	T	O		D	I	R	G	E				
			B	E	T	T	E	M	I	D	L	E	R	
			K	U	R	T	Z			E	L	A	N	D
G	R	R		S	A	C		W	A	D		I	C	E
R	A	I	S	E	S	H	E	E	P		S	N	O	W
A	M	B	U	S	H		L	A	P	S	E	D		
S	P	A	R		C	A	L	L	T	O	A	R	M	S
S	E	L	F		A	L	I	T		F	L	O	O	R
O	D	D	S		N	A	S	H		T	Y	P	E	A

50

S	A	I	L		E	L	E	V		L	O	G	A	N
M	U	L	E		L	O	B	E		I	V	A	N	A
E	L	L	A		D	E	A	N		V	A	L	E	T
L	A	I	D	D	O	W	N	T	H	E	L	A	W	
T	I	N		E	R	E		I	A	N				
S	T	I	G	M	A		O	L	D		W	E	A	K
			E	U	D	O	R	A		H	O	R	D	E
P	O	W	E	R	O	F	A	T	T	O	R	N	E	Y
A	N	I	S	E		F	L	E	E	T	S			
N	O	N	E		C	C	S		A	T	E	A	S	E
			A	P	E		D	R	U		M	T	A	
	C	O	P	S	A	N	D	R	O	B	B	E	R	S
L	O	P	E	S		T	O	E	S		A	L	I	T
O	C	A	L	A		E	D	G	E		R	I	P	E
S	A	L	T	Y		R	O	S	S		B	A	E	R

51

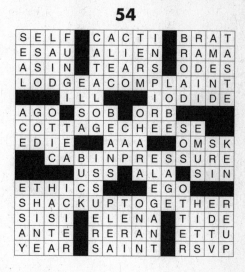

C	O	M	A	■	T	B	I	L	L	■	B	L	A	B
A	D	A	M	■	O	L	L	I	E	■	L	O	S	E
T	I	N	A	L	O	U	I	S	E	■	A	N	T	E
S	E	X	■	O	T	R	A	■	I	D	E	A	S	■
■	■	B	O	B	D	E	N	V	E	R	■	■	■	■
B	O	O	H	O	O	■	■	R	I	I	S	■	■	■
E	L	I	A	■	C	E	A	S	E	■	B	A	A	■
G	I	L	L	I	G	A	N	S	I	S	L	A	N	D
S	O	Y	■	M	A	R	G	E	■	O	L	D	E	■
■	■	M	A	R	T	■	P	A	N	D	A	S	■	■
■	J	I	M	B	A	C	K	U	S	■	■	■	■	■
F	A	U	N	S	■	L	E	S	E	■	A	A	A	■
I	M	I	N	■	A	L	A	N	H	A	L	E	J	R
T	A	C	O	■	H	O	R	D	E	■	A	R	A	T
S	T	E	W	■	S	T	O	O	D	■	D	O	R	Y

52

A	L	F	A	■	E	L	B	O	W	■	S	H	A	M
T	A	R	S	■	R	E	E	C	E	■	H	A	T	E
K	N	E	W	■	N	I	G	H	T	C	O	U	R	T
A	D	E	A	L	■	S	I	R	■	A	R	T	I	E
■	M	A	N	O	F	■	N	E	W	S	T	E	P	S
Z	I	G	■	P	E	N	N	■	E	E	L	■	■	■
O	N	E	R	■	R	O	I	L	S	■	I	F	S	O
L	E	N	A	■	R	U	N	A	T	■	S	O	N	S
A	S	T	I	■	A	N	G	I	E	■	T	O	O	L
■	■	N	C	R	■	O	R	N	O	■	T	W	O	■
M	I	S	C	H	I	E	F	■	D	R	I	F	T	■
O	M	A	H	A	■	C	F	O	■	G	R	A	I	L
W	A	T	E	R	G	L	A	S	S	■	A	U	R	A
E	R	I	C	■	S	A	L	S	A	■	N	L	E	R
R	I	N	K	■	A	T	L	A	S	■	I	T	S	A

53

S	T	E	M	■	S	T	A	B	■	C	E	D	A	R
S	O	U	R	■	H	E	R	O	■	A	L	I	V	E
T	E	R	M	■	E	R	G	O	■	N	A	K	E	D
■	S	O	O	N	E	R	O	R	L	A	T	E	R	■
■	■	M	O	N	O	■	O	R	E	■	■	■	■	■
R	A	M	■	V	A	R	S	I	T	Y	■	G	P	A
A	T	O	N	E	■	A	N	T	■	F	R	A	N	■
D	O	U	B	L	E	O	R	N	O	T	H	I	N	G
I	L	S	A	■	P	O	D	■	O	A	T	E	R	■
O	L	E	■	A	C	H	I	E	S	T	■	S	L	Y
■	■	G	T	O	■	N	E	E	D	■	■	■	■	■
■	F	E	A	S	T	O	R	F	A	M	I	N	E	■
A	L	E	U	T	■	P	O	O	L	■	T	O	B	E
L	O	N	G	U	■	E	L	L	E	■	S	N	A	G
K	E	Y	E	D	■	R	E	D	D	■	Y	O	Y	O

54

S	E	L	F	■	C	A	C	T	I	■	B	R	A	T
E	S	A	U	■	A	L	I	E	N	■	R	A	M	A
A	S	I	N	■	T	E	A	R	S	■	O	D	E	S
L	O	D	G	E	A	C	O	M	P	L	A	I	N	T
■	■	■	I	L	L	■	■	I	O	D	I	D	E	■
A	G	O	■	S	O	B	■	O	R	B	■	■	■	■
C	O	T	T	A	G	E	C	H	E	E	S	E	■	■
E	D	I	E	■	■	A	A	A	■	■	O	M	S	K
■	■	C	A	B	I	N	P	R	E	S	S	U	R	E
■	■	■	U	S	S	■	A	L	A	■	S	I	N	■
E	T	H	I	C	S	■	■	■	E	G	O	■	■	■
S	H	A	C	K	U	P	T	O	G	E	T	H	E	R
S	I	S	I	■	E	L	E	N	A	■	T	I	D	E
A	N	T	E	■	R	E	R	A	N	■	E	T	T	U
Y	E	A	R	■	S	A	I	N	T	■	R	S	V	P

55

A	S	I	A	N	■	W	I	F	E	■	A	S	I	S
L	O	N	G	A	■	I	T	E	R	■	G	I	V	E
T	B	A	R	S	■	N	O	L	O	■	O	N	Y	X
H	E	W	A	S	A	G	O	O	D	E	G	G	■	■
O	R	E	■	A	L	S	■	N	E	H	■	A	S	S
■	■	H	U	M	P	T	Y	D	U	M	P	T	Y	■
A	C	T	I	■	A	A	A	■	■	D	O	O	R	S
G	A	W	K	■	S	N	I	D	E	■	P	R	A	T
G	R	I	E	G	■	L	U	I	■	U	E	Y	S	■
I	T	C	R	A	C	K	S	M	E	U	P	■	■	■
E	E	E	■	B	O	A	■	P	I	N	■	T	A	G
■	■	T	H	E	O	V	A	L	O	F	F	I	C	E
A	M	O	I	■	I	N	R	I	■	U	R	B	A	N
O	I	L	S	■	N	E	O	N	■	R	E	E	S	E
L	A	D	S	■	G	R	O	G	■	L	Y	R	E	S

56

```
S W E P T   A J A R   S I P S
P A T I O   N O P E   T N U T
A D A G E   E K E D   R A R A
      S H O W E R S H O W E R
S K I T O W       A V E R T
M O B I L E M O B I L E
E A S E D   I M O F F   C P R
A L E S   P A N T S   S H O O
R A N   C O M I C   C O A S T
      P O L I S H P O L I S H
C L E A N         E N U R E S
A U G U S T A U G U S T
R A Y S   E X P O   O I L E D
D U P E   A L T O   L O T T O
S S T S   L E O N   E N R O N
```

57

```
B L A B S   F A R E D   A B C
A U D I T   I M B R O G L I O
S N I D E   L O I N C L O T H
I C E   A C L U     S O T T O
C H U C K B E R R Y   B A Y S
      U S S   E A S E L
R O I L   A I S L E   I Z E
R U M P E L S T I L T S K I N
S T P   L E T O N   W E P T
    R E F E R   A L A
A T O N   R O U N D A B O U T
L O V E S   T O O T   G N U
P R I M E C U T S   H E L I X
E A S Y T O S E E   A R E T E
S H E   H E A R D   M A R E S
```

58

```
L E G S   H I T I T   B A S S
A L O T   A N I S E   A R C O
H O W A R D K E E L   Y E A R
R I N G O   D E L A W A R E
      G A Z A   A B A
A C E   D A N I E L S T E R N
D U N   S P I R A L   C L U E
H O S T   M I T   H U N T
O M O O   P A S S E S   D O W
C O R D E L L H U L L   E N T
    I R A   P I A F
G R E E N T E A   S L E E T
L O A F   O R R I N H A T C H
I M S O   O G I V E   P A R E
B E E R   N O D E D   S T U N
```

59

```
D I S C   S M A S H   A S P S
U T A H   E S T E E   S P A M
C O M E O N D O W N   S I N E
      A M O O N   P L U N G E
B U T T E R S   C A I R O
A T H E N S   B A R T E R E D
D O E R   N O R T H   S S E
E P A   G O O D B Y E   O P S
G I N   O B O E S   A L I A
G A S M A S K S   M A R V E L
    W I P E S   F O R R E S T
C R E M E S   E A T M E
H E R O   S U R V E Y S A Y S
I B I S   E A S E L   T R A Y
N A S A   D R E S S   S K Y S
```

60

```
A M A H S   S C A P E   A B A
L O G A N   E L I A S   N O W
A T R I A   R U N T S   D N A
S H A R K T E E T H   E R I K
      N E O N   E F F E T E
S L U E   W A Y S T A T I O N
S O F T G   E P I C S
T O O   R E E N A C T   A M I
    F A U S T   S E V E N
H O P E F L O A T S   Y A N K
U S E D T O   E A S E
B I T S   G R E A T W H I T E
C R U   R I O T S   I O N I C
A I L   O Z O N E   G L I N T
P S A   B E T A S   S E T T O
```

61

```
P A D S . A S S A M . . T H D .
E L E C . N I T R O . R E I N .
A L F A . T R U E R . O H N O .
C H I L L I E R W E A T H E R .
H E A D Y . . M E N U . E D U .
E R N . S I E . O R P H A N .
S E T S . A N E S . A S S T S .
. . . W I L D G E E S E . . .
S C R A M . S G T S . C A D S .
C H U M P S . H S T . N A H .
O I D . E A S E . W A C K Y .
F L O R I D A V A C A T I O N .
F I L A . D R I V E . T E T E .
S E P T . L A C E D . I N A S .
. S H E . E N T R E . C T N S .
```

62

```
O N R Y E . S A R A N . D A B
B A C O N . E L O P E . I G O
S H A K E S P E A R E . L A W
. . E M O T E D . S M A Z E .
D U B L I N . S C O O P E R .
O S U . E Y E S . A N N I .
G U L F S . A T M S . I D E A
M A L L . F R U I T . C A R T
A L F A . O L D S . N A T A L
. I N C A . Y O G A . E S A
B I G G A M E . A S I D E S .
O T H E R . V A U L T S . .
R A T . H A I R R A I S I N G
O L E . O R L O N . E U R O S
N O R . P E S O S . R E A T A
```

63

```
K E E L . R A M P S . A F A R
N Y S E . I D E A L . B O L O
O R S O N B E A N O . O N T O
T E E N I E S T . M U Z A K .
. . I C Y . A T I T . . .
N O P . K E N O G R I F F E Y
A M A S S . O R E O . A L E E
B A L I . S T O N Y . C O R A
O N I N . P A N T . L E W I S
B I N G O C R O S B Y . N E T
. A D A Y . A S K . . .
G R A P E . E S T O N I A N
O U Z O . T R E N T L O T T O
O D O R . A U R A L . W C T U
N E V E . G R O P E . S H U N
```

64

```
S C A L P . A M I S . A D A M
T A L E S . P A S T . S A G O
A L L A H . O S L O . L R O N
M I C H A E L K E A T O N .
E P A . W A L E . S U P E R B
N E S S . S O D A . F E R I A
. R H E T T . F I A T . S O T
. . V A L K I L M E R . .
M I R . T A I L . O D E L L
A D A P T . A M E R . M E O W
N I N E O F . H O A X . O R R
. G E O R G E C L O O N E Y
J E E R . Y O R E . U T I L E
A T R A . E T O N . T O N E S
W E S T . R O S E . S E E I T
```

65

```
T A T A . O N U S . P R A D O
O B I T . F E S T . R E S I N
M E E T S F A C E T O F A C E
S T R I P . G R A F . P E A
. . L A N E . E M I L . .
. S T A N D S T O E T O T O E
A L I . K A T E . S N A R L
L E A N . K E E P S . G R A M
P E R O N . N E A L . D T S
S T A R E S E Y E T O E Y E .
. . A M I N . R E G S . .
A B E . E G G S . A C H O O
W A L K S H A N D I N H A N D
A D L A I . G O O D . E L I E
Y E A T S . E W E S . W E T S
```

66

W	H	O	A		M	O	S	A	I	C	
	U	L	E								

66

```
WHOA  MOSAIC  ULE
HINT  OPENTO  HAT
ITEM  BALDERDASH
GAS  KILLS  SOUSA
  SEOUL  REVLON
BLATHERSKITE
OUTIN  EPICS  TIP
AMES  RHINO  CONE
SPR  DEALT  LANCE
  GOBBLEDYGOOK
ERRATA  ONEAM
LOOSE  PEACE  VEG
FLAPDOODLE  MATE
IFS  OREGON  GIAN
NET  NOTYET  MLXX
```

67

```
FROG  SABOT  POPS
RIMA  AGORA  OREL
ONOR  TOTAL  TIRE
 GOBLINONESFOOD
   ONYX  PUNTS
ELSIE  URAL
SANDWITCHES  DUB
SHOO  GUION  PERO
ORB  HOTGHOULASH
   PERU  POLAR
PEALE  ASIT
ELFELFASPROUTS
RATA  INTRO  ROAD
ETES  SKEIN  DRNO
SERE  CARTS  UNDO
```

68

```
PRIM  GERM  TOAST
OONA  ELIA  OLLIE
OMAN  TALC  PESOS
LETITALLHANGOUT
 RANG  ONO  PXS
ASA  TRES  STP
RUNS  IDLY  CONGA
KICKUPYOURHEELS
STEIN  SEMI  TAUT
  NCO °SAPS  TEA
SCH  UPS  COIF
PAINTTHETOWNRED
IDTAG  ODOR  TEAR
TEMPE  READ  RAVE
STEAM  ENDS  OKED
```

69

```
SHIV  APPT  RECAP
AERO  CLUE  ERUPT
GNAT  CANDIDATES
ARTISTIC  RNS
SIENA  THYME  ALI
  GNU  COACHMEN
ASIS  SOAK  KABOB
DELI  SPREE  NENE
DELTA  IDLE  GRAD
TIGERCUB  LEI
ONO  MAMAS  ANGUS
  ORR  LASTGASP
ATTHEPOLLS  CLEO
LOUIS  LOST  HAUT
BEGOT  ETAS  ASPS
             D
```

70

```
COLIC  BELG  VEDA
LAURA  OPER  SAUD
ATTAR  LICE  IVES
WHENONECHANGES
  UAR  TEN
LANESTOGOFASTER
ELITE  ABUT  AVE
ALEE  KAREN  SPEC
PAC  GARB  SPIRO
THELANEONEWASIN
  EEG  ESE
 WILLACCELERATE
PICA  RAID  POSIT
UPON  ORAL  ENTER
TEND  OBOE  RAISE
```

71

```
L Y N X   P S S T   S T A R E
B E A M   E C H O   E A S E L
S A N E   R O A M   A R I E L
  H A N D O N H A N D O F F S
    O N E   H O O T
D E C A Y S   H A I G   T A P
A L A M O   S E W S   L O G O
T A K E U P T A K E D O W N S
U T E S   O A R S   I V I E S
M E D   S P I T   T S E T S E
    S T I R   T A C
W O R K I N W O R K O U T S
A L I E N   A L E E   C O O L
S L E E T   Y E A R   L U R E
P A N T S   S O T S   A R E A
```

72

```
S P A M   S N O B   A T A L E
A L S O   W A R E   R O L E X
S A I L   A R C H   A B A T E
H I D D E N C H A R G E S
A D E S T E   R O O
      H E A D   K N O W E R
D U A N E   T I N E   R I T A
U N D E R C O V E R A G E N T
M E I N   A P E R   M Y N A S
A S T E R N   R O B O
      E S Q   I N T E R S
  C A M O U F L A G E N E T
J O Y C E   I R I S   N E M O
A H A R D   R A Z E   T R I O
M O N E Y   E T A S   H O T L
```

73

```
O R S   B A S S   W I S P S
M E T S   E S T E   O S H E A
I D E A   T H E C U R S E O F
T S P S   R O W   S L O A N E
  C S T A R   H E D   R Y S
A S H   E Y E   O R S O
L A I R D S   B A S E B A L L
A L L O W   S O X   R O M E O
R E D B I R D S   T I E S T O
    E L E A   P R E   T S K
M A P   L A K   H E S S E
E C L A I R   M O M   A R C S
T H E B A M B I N O   A D U E
R E A L M   I C E R   B A B E
E S S E S   B E D S   M S S
```

74

```
I C E S   B A L M   S W O R E
D I S H   E S A U   M A Y O R
E N T R   A C D C   O G L E R
A C E I N T H E H O L E
L O R N A       O R D   A S A
    K I N G O F B E A S T S
I F S   L A I R   R O S E S
R O O F   M A D A M   L E N A
A C R E S   E D A M   T O Y
Q U E E N F O R A D A Y
I S R   E T A   Y E A S T
    J A C K B E N I M B L E
N O V A K   L A M E   E B A N
O X I D E   E L M S   N E T S
D O Z E R   Y E A S   I S E E
```

75

```
B E S T   O N E N D   C E D E
A R N O   R U M O R   O M A R
Y O U M U S T B E J O K I N G
H O B B S   M A S   B I L K O
      O P E S   F E E
W H E N P I G S F L Y   P L O
H A R D E R   Y A O   I S A Y
A L M A N A C   T R A S H T V
L E A K   N O D   I N T A K E
E S S   T H E R E S N O W A Y
      A H A   A N T I
A D I E U   A G R   K I O S K
A I N T G O N N A H A P P E N
R E I N   D I E G O   S A N E
E T T A   E S T E E   O L D E
```

The New York Times

Crossword Puzzles

The #1 name in crosswords

Coming Soon!

Holiday Cheer Crossword Puzzles	0-312-36126-2	$11.95/$15.95
Carefree Crosswords	0-312-36102-5	$6.95/$9.95
Groovy Crosswords from the 60s	0-312-36103-3	$6.95/$9.95
Supersized Sunday Crosswords	0-312-36122-X	$15.95/$21.95
Large Print Omnibus Vol. 7	0-312-36125-4	$11.95/$15.95
Daily Omnibus Vol. 16	0-312-36104-1	$11.95/$15.95
Little Black (and White) Book of Crosswords	0-312-36105-X	$12.95/$17.95
Will Shortz Presents Crosswords for 365 Days	0-312-36121-1	$8.95/$13.95
Easy Omnibus Vol. 5	0-312-36123-8	$11.95/$15.95
Everyday Sunday	0-312-36106-8	$6.95/$9.95
Sunday Crossword Puzzles Vol.32	0-312-36066-5	$9.95/$13.95

Special Editions

Brainbuilder Crosswords	0-312-35276-X	$6.95/$9.95 Can.
Fitness for the Mind Crosswords Vol. 2	0-312-35278-6	$10.95/$14.95 Can.
Vocabulary Power Crosswords	0-312-35199-2	$10.95/$14.95 Can.
Will Shortz Xtreme Xwords	0-312-35203-4	$6.95/$9.95 Can.
Will Shortz's Greatest Hits	0-312-34242-X	$8.95/$12.95 Can.
Super Sunday Crosswords	0-312-33115-0	$10.95/$15.95 Can.
Will Shortz's Funniest Crosswords Vol. 2	0-312-33960-7	$9.95/$13.95 Can.
Will Shortz's Funniest Crosswords	0-312-32489-8	$9.95/$14.95 Can.
Will Shortz's Sunday Favorites	0-312-32488-X	$9.95/$14.95 Can.
Crosswords for a Brain Workout	0-312-32610-6	$6.95/$9.95 Can.
Crosswords to Boost Your Brainpower	0-312-32033-7	$6.95/$9.95 Can.
Crossword All-Stars	0-312-31004-8	$9.95/$14.95 Can.
Will Shortz's Favorites	0-312-30613-X	$9.95/$14.95 Can.
Ultimate Omnibus	0-312-31622-4	$17.95/$25.95 Can.

Daily Crosswords

Daily Crossword puzzles Vol. 72	0-312-35260-3	$10.95/$14.95 Can.
Fitness for the Mind Vol. 1	0-312-34955-6	$10.95/$14.95 Can.
Crosswords for the Weekend	0-312-34332-9	$9.95/$14.95 Can.
Monday through Friday Vol. 2	0-312-31459-0	$9.95/$14.95 Can.
Monday through Friday	0-312-30058-1	$9.95/$14.95 Can.
Daily Crosswords Vol. 71	0-312-34858-4	$9.95/$14.95 Can.
Daily Crosswords Vol. 70	0-312-34239-X	$9.95/$14.95 Can.
Daily Crosswords Vol. 69	0-312-33956-9	$9.95/$14.95 Can.
Daily Crosswords Vol. 68	0-312-33434-6	$9.95/$14.95 Can.
Daily Crosswords Vol. 67	0-312-32437-5	$9.95/$14.95 Can.
Daily Crosswords Vol. 66	0-312-32436-7	$9.95/$14.95 Can.
Daily Crosswords Vol. 65	0-312-32034-5	$9.95/$14.95 Can.
Daily Crosswords Vol. 64	0-312-31458-2	$9.95/$14.95 Can.

Volumes 57–63 also available

Easy Crosswords

Easy Crosswords Puzzles Vol. 7	0-312-35261-1	$9.95/$14.95 Can.
Easy Crosswords Vol. 6	0-312-33957-7	$10.95/$15.95 Can.
Easy Crosswords Vol. 5	0-312-32438-3	$9.95/$14.95 Can.

Volumes 2–4 also available

Tough Crosswords

Tough Crosswords Vol. 13	0-312-34240-3	$10.95/$14.95 Can.
Tough Crosswords Vol. 12	0-312-32442-1	$10.95/$14.95 Can.
Tough Crosswords Vol. 11	0-312-31456-6	$10.95/$15.95 Can.

Volumes 9–10 also available

Sunday Crosswords

Sunday Morning Crossword Puzzles	0-312-35672-2	$6.95/$9.95 Can.
Sunday in the Park Crosswords	0-312-35197-6	$6.95/$9.95 Can.
Sunday Crosswords Vol. 30	0-312-33538-5	$9.95/$14.95 Can.
Sunday Crosswords Vol. 29	0-312-32038-8	$9.95/$14.95 Can.
Sunday Crosswords Vol. 28	0-312-30515-X	$9.95/$14.95 Can.
Sunday Crosswords Vol. 27	0-312-20414-4	$9.95/$14.95 Can.

Large-Print Crosswords

Large-Print Crosswords for Your Bedside	0-312-34245-4	$10.95/$14.95 Can.
Large-Print Will Shortz's Favorite Crosswords	0-312-33959-3	$10.95/$15.95 Can.
Large-Print Big Book of Easy Crosswords	0-312-33958-5	$12.95/$18.95 Can.
Large-Print Big Book of Holiday Crosswords	0-312-33092-8	$12.95/$18.95 Can.
Large-Print Crosswords for Your Coffeebreak	0-312-33109-6	$10.95/$15.95 Can.

Large-Print Crosswords for a Brain Workout	0-312-32612-2	$10.95/$15.95 Can.
Large Print Crosswords to Boost Your Brainpower	0-312-32037-X	$11.95/$17.95 Can.
Large-Print Easy Omnibus	0-312-32439-1	$12.95/$18.95 Can.
Large-Print Daily Crosswords Vol. 2	0-312-33111-8	$10.95/$15.95 Can.
Large-Print Daily Crosswords	0-312-31457-4	$10.95/$15.95 Can.
Large-Print Omnibus Vol.6	0-312-34861-4	$12.95/$18.95 Can.
Large-Print Omnibus Vol. 5	0-312-32036-1	$12.95/$18.95 Can.

Previous volumes also available

Omnibus

Biggest Beach Crossword Omnibus	0-312-35667-6	$11.95/$15.95 Can.
Weekend Away Crossword Puzzle Omnibus	0-312-35669-2	$11.95/$15.95 Can.
Weekend at Home Crossword Puzzle Omnibus	0-312-35670-6	$11.95/$15.95 Can.
Sunday Crossword Omnibus Volume 9	0-312-35666-8	$11.95/$17.95 Can.
Lazy Sunday Crossword Puzzle Omnibus	0-312-35279-4	$11.95/$15.95 Can.
Crosswords for a Weekend Getaway	0-312-35198-4	$11.95/$15.95 Can.
Supersized Book of Easy Crosswords	0-312-35277-8	$14.95/$21.95 Can.
Crossword Challenge	0-312-33951-8	$12.95/$18.95 Can.
Giant Book of Holiday Crosswords	0-312-34927-0	$11.95/$15.95 Can.
Big Book of Holiday Crosswords	0-312-33533-4	$11.95/$16.95 Can.
Lazy Weekend Crosswords	0-312-34247-0	$11.95/$15.95 Can.
Crosswords for a Lazy Afternoon	0-312-33108-8	$11.95/$17.95 Can.
Tough Omnibus Vol. 1	0-312-34441-3	$11.95/$17.95 Can.
Easy Omnibus Vol. 4	0-312-34859-2	$11.95/$17.95 Can.
Easy Omnibus Vol. 3	0-312-33537-7	$11.95/$17.95 Can.
Easy Omnibus Vol. 2	0-312-32035-3	$11.95/$17.95 Can.
Easy Omnibus Vol. 1	0-312-30513-3	$11.95/$17.95 Can.
Daily Omnibus Vol. 15	0-312-34856-8	$11.95/$17.95 Can.
Daily Omnibus Vol. 14	0-312-33534-2	$11.95/$17.95 Can.
Daily Omnibus Vol. 13	0-312-32031-0	$11.95/$17.95 Can.
Sunday Omnibus Vol. 8	0-312-32440-5	$11.95/$17.95 Can.
Sunday Omnibus Vol. 7	0-312-30950-3	$11.95/$17.95 Can.
Sunday Omnibus Vol. 6	0-312-28913-8	$11.95/$17.95 Can.

Variety Puzzles

Acrostic Puzzles Vol. 10	0-312-34853-3	$9.95/$14.95 Can.
Acrostic Puzzles Vol. 9	0-312-30949-X	$9.95/$14.95 Can.
Sunday Variety Puzzles	0-312-30059-X	$9.95/$14.95 Can.

Previous volumes also available

Portable Size Format

Easy Crossword Puzzles for Lazy Hazy Crazy Days	0-312-35671-4	$6.95/$9.95 Can.
Backyard Crossword Puzzles	0-312-35668-4	$6.95/$9.95 Can.
Fast and Easy Crossword Puzzles	0-312-35629-3	$6.95/$9.95 Can.
Crosswords for Your Lunch Hour	0-312-34857-6	$6.95/$9.95 Can.
Café Crosswords	0-312-34854-1	$6.95/$9.95 Can.
Easy as Pie Crosswords	0-312-34331-0	$6.95/$9.95 Can.
More Quick Crosswords	0-312-34246-2	$6.95/$9.95 Can.
Crosswords to Soothe Your Soul	0-312-34244-6	$6.95/$9.95 Can.
Beach Blanket Crosswords	0-312-34250-0	$6.95/$9.95 Can.
Simply Sunday Crosswords	0-312-34243-8	$6.95/$9.95 Can.
Crosswords for a Rainy Day	0-312-33952-6	$6.95/$9.95 Can.
Crosswords for Stress Relief	0-312-33953-4	$6.95/$9.95 Can.
Crosswords to Beat the Clock	0-312-33954-2	$6.95/$9.95 Can.
Quick Crosswords	0-312-33114-2	$6.95/$9.95 Can.
More Sun, Sand and Crosswords	0-312-33112-6	$6.95/$9.95 Can.
Planes, Trains and Crosswords	0-312-33113-4	$6.95/$9.95 Can.
Cup of Tea and Crosswords	0-312-32435-9	$6.95/$9.95 Can.
Crosswords for Your Bedside	0-312-32032-9	$6.95/$9.95 Can.
Beach Bag Crosswords	0-312-31455-8	$6.95/$9.95 Can.
T.G.I.F. Crosswords	0-312-33116-9	$6.95/$9.95 Can.
Super Saturday	0-312-30604-0	$6.95/$9.95 Can.

Other volumes also available

For Young Solvers

New York Times on the Web Crosswords for Teens	0-312-28911-1	$6.95/$9.95 Can.
Outrageous Crossword Puzzles and Word Games for Kids	0-312-28915-1	$6.95/$9.95 Can.
More Outrageous Crossword Puzzles for Kids	0-312-30062-X	$6.95/$9.95 Can.

St. Martin's Griffin